DIABETIC
Diet COOKBOOK
After 50

BONUS INSIDE

60-DAY MEAL PLAN

Nourish Your Body,
Control Your Diabetes

1000 Days

of Easy Recipes and Balanced Nutrition for
Pre-Diabetes and Type 2 Diabetes
Management

Lara Rush

Table of Contents

DIABETES: WHAT IT IS?

Diabetes is a chronic condition caused by insufficient production of insulin by the pancreas or its inadequate utilization. Insulin is the hormone responsible for regulating blood glucose levels; individuals with diabetes accumulate glucose in their blood.

Types of diabetes

1. Type 1 diabetes is triggered by the immune system attacking the pancreatic cells that produce insulin. It can occur at any age, although it commonly develops in children and adolescents and requires daily insulin treatment.
2. Type 2 diabetes results from either reduced insulin production by the pancreas or the body's resistance to insulin. It is often associated with obesity and a sedentary lifestyle, hence treated through lifestyle and dietary changes. This condition is prevalent among adults and adolescents suffering from obesity.
3. Another common type is gestational diabetes, which occurs during pregnancy but increases the risk of developing type 2 diabetes later on.

Diagnosis

The criteria for diagnosing diabetes include:
- Symptoms of diabetes (polyuria, polydipsia, unexplained weight loss) associated with a random blood glucose level, regardless of the time of day, ≥ 200 mg/dL.

OR
- Fasting blood glucose level ≥ 126 mg/dL. Fasting is defined as the absence of food intake for at least 8 hours.

OR
- Blood glucose ≥ 200 mg/dL during an oral glucose tolerance test (OGTT). The test should be performed by administering 75 g of glucose.

OR
- Glycated hemoglobin (HbA1c) higher than 6.5% (or 48 mmol/mol) (see below). Additionally, there are clinical situations where blood glucose does not exceed the defined levels for diabetes, yet they do not represent a normal condition. In these cases, it is referred to as Impaired Fasting Glucose (IFG) when fasting glucose values range between 100 and 125 mg/dL, and Impaired Glucose Tolerance (IGT) when blood glucose two hours after a glucose load is between 140 and 200 mg/dL. These conditions indicate a high risk of developing diabetes even though they do not constitute a disease state. They are often associated with overweight, dyslipidemia, and/or hypertension, leading to an increased risk of cardiovascular events.

Complications of diabetes

Diabetes can lead to acute or chronic complications. Acute complications are more common in type 1 diabetes and are related to the almost total lack of insulin. In these cases, the patient may experience ketoacidotic coma due to the accumulation of altered metabolism products, ketones, causing unconsciousness, dehydration, and severe blood disturbances.

In type 2 diabetes, acute complications are rare, while chronic complications affecting various organs and tissues, including the eyes, kidneys, heart, blood vessels, and peripheral nerves, are more frequent.

- **Diabetic retinopathy:** Damage to small blood vessels supplying the retina, resulting in visual impairment. Diabetic individuals are also more prone to developing eye diseases such as glaucoma and cataracts.
- **Diabetic nephropathy:** A progressive reduction in kidney filtration function that, if untreated, can lead to renal failure, requiring dialysis and/or kidney transplantation.
- **Cardiovascular diseases:** The risk of cardiovascular diseases is 2 to 4 times higher in people with diabetes than in the general population, causing over 50% of diabetes-related deaths in industrialized countries.

Risk factors

Chronic complications of diabetes can be prevented or their progression slowed through strict control of all related risk factors.

- Blood glucose and glycated hemoglobin (HbA1c): Important clinical studies emphasize the significance of good metabolic control in preventing complications. Average glucose levels throughout the day can be assessed by measuring glycated hemoglobin (HbA1c%). In diabetic patients,

This underscores the need to consider cardiovascular risk in diabetic patients equivalent to those who have experienced a cardiovascular event.

- **Diabetic neuropathy:** One of the most common complications, occurring at different levels in 50% of diabetics, according to the World Health Organization. It can cause loss of sensitivity, varying degrees of pain, and limb damage, necessitating amputation in severe cases. It can lead to dysfunction in the heart, eyes, stomach, and is a major cause of male impotence.
- **Diabetic foot:** Changes in the structure of blood vessels and nerves can lead to ulcers and problems in the lower limbs, especially the feet, due to the loads they bear. This statistically constitutes the leading cause of non-traumatic lower limb amputation.
- **Pregnancy complications:** In pregnant women, diabetes can result in adverse outcomes for the fetus, from congenital malformations to high birth weight and a higher risk of perinatal mortality.

this value must be kept below 7% to be considered in "good metabolic control."

- Blood pressure: Diabetics have an increased risk of cardiovascular disease, making blood pressure control crucial, as elevated levels already represent a risk factor. Blood pressure control can prevent the onset of cardiovascular diseases (heart diseases and strokes) and microcirculation-related conditions (eyes, kidneys, and the nervous system).
- Blood lipid control: Dyslipidemias also represent an additional risk factor for

cardiovascular diseases. Adequate control of cholesterol and lipids (HDL, LDL, and triglycerides) can reduce the onset of cardiovascular complications, especially in patients who have already experienced a cardiovascular event.

Given the high frequency of vascular complications, close monitoring of target organs (eyes, kidneys, and lower limbs) is imperative. Therefore, individuals with diabetes should undergo regular check-ups, even in the absence of symptoms.

Therapeutic interventions

The cornerstone of diabetic disease therapy revolves around adopting a suitable lifestyle. Lifestyle encompasses dietary habits, physical activity, and smoking cessation.

The diet for individuals with diabetes (referred to in the USA as Medical Nutrition Therapy) aims to reduce the risk of diabetes complications and cardiovascular diseases by maintaining blood glucose and lipid levels, as well as blood pressure, as close to normal as possible.

In general, it is recommended that the diet includes carbohydrates from fruits, vegetables, grains, legumes, and skimmed milk, not falling below 130 g/day. It is essential to ensure balanced intake through measurement and alternative use. Avoid the use of sucrose, substituting it with sweeteners. Similar to the general population, consuming fiber-containing foods is advised. Regarding fats, it is crucial to limit their intake to <7% of total daily calories, with particular emphasis on saturated fats and cholesterol.

Aerobic and moderately intense physical activity for at least 150 minutes per week, or more intense activity for 90 minutes per

week, is recommended to improve glycemic control and maintain body weight. This activity should be distributed over at least three times a week, with no more than two consecutive days without activity. Similar to the general population, avoiding smoking is advised, with smoking cessation support included as part of diabetes treatment.

Type 1 diabetics require tighter regulation of insulin therapy in accordance with dietary intake and physical activity. For type 2 diabetics, who are generally overweight or obese, an adequate lifestyle, including calorie reduction, especially from fats, and increased physical activity, takes on greater importance to improve blood glucose, dyslipidemia, and blood pressure levels.

Why choose a diabetic diet: dietary goals and nutritional advice

The primary objectives of a diabetes-friendly diet include:

- Glycemic control
- Body weight management
- Lipid level control
- Prevention and treatment of nutrition-related risk factors or complications.

For this reason, we will suggest a diet suitable for you who live with this pathology. You will learn to eat well, without putting your health at risk. We will recommend tasty recipes, in doses for two people, to easily make at home.

CHAPTER 1: TRICKS FOR A BALANCED DIET: HOW TO DIVIDE NUTRIENTS THROUGHOUT THE DAY

A balanced diet

Maintaining good health involves adapting the quantity of food consumed to achieve and sustain an ideal weight throughout one's life. Therefore, a balance between portions, food quality, and daily physical activity is essential. The success of a program is sometimes achieved through small tricks:

- Planning meals in advance prevents impulsive consumption of high-fat options (such as cheese, cold cuts, etc.).
- Eating slowly is crucial; those who eat quickly tend to consume more. Chewing slowly helps to better recognize the feeling of satiety.
- Listening to one's body is key: is it genuine hunger or simply boredom?
- Portion control is important; preparing one's portion and storing leftovers (keeping them off the table makes it less tempting to consume them).
- Eating regularly by consuming measured portions and incorporating planned, healthy snacks (such as a piece of fruit or low-fat yogurt) throughout the day prevents excessive hunger at the next meal.

Balancing food intake with the level of physical activity: if no physical activity occurs during the day, consuming less is advisable.

The optimal diet consists of a balanced, varied, and nutritious diet. Introducing foods in the right proportions is crucial, focusing on:

- Proteins (10 - 20%)
- Fats (20 - 35%)
- Carbohydrates (45 - 60%)

The fundamental concept of a healthy diet is the diversity of food intake while meeting energy needs. Carbohydrates serve as the primary energy source, aiming to provide about half of the total daily caloric intake.

Carbohydrates

Carbohydrates are classified into simple and complex categories. Simple sugars should constitute no more than approximately 10% of total daily caloric intake. Found in table sugar, sweets, honey, fruit, milk, jam, and sugary beverages, these sugars are often associated with high fat content, low vitamin and mineral levels (as seen in sweets), offering minimal nutritional value.

Complex sugars make up the remaining caloric portion and are present in bread, pasta, breadsticks, crackers, toast, rice, legumes, and potatoes. Be cautious with **"sugar-free"** or **"diet"** products, as their energy content is often similar to that of regular products.

Fiber

For a well-balanced diet, it is beneficial to increase the intake of fiber. The goal is to consume approximately 20 grams per 1000 Kcal. Fibers are plant components that give them their shape and are not absorbed into the bloodstream. There are two types of fibers:

- **Soluble fibers:** These dissolve in water and have a gummy consistency that helps lower cholesterol levels and control blood glucose, thereby protecting against diabetes and cardiovascular diseases.
- **Insoluble fibers:** These do not dissolve in water but are valuable for regulating the intestines and preventing constipation.

If one is not accustomed to incorporating fiber into the diet, it is advisable to do so gradually to avoid gas formation and a sense of bloating.

A useful strategy is to replace white flour bread and pasta with whole-grain alternatives. The table below provides examples of foods rich in soluble and insoluble fibers:

SOLUBLE FIBER	INSOLUBLE FIBER
Legumes	Bran (rice, oats, barley, wheat)
Fruits (apples, oranges, pears, peaches, grapes)	Vegetables (carrots, potatoes, squash, corn)
Berries (blackberries, raspberries, prunes)	Whole grains (bread, cereals, pasta)

Including a variety of these fiber-rich foods in your diet supports overall health and helps achieve the recommended daily fiber intake.

Fats

Fats provide the body with reserve energy stored in adipose tissue. They should constitute a maximum of 35% of the calories in our diet, with saturated fats not exceeding 10%.

Proteins

Proteins are essential substances for our body, and in the absence of renal complications, we should intake approximately 1 gram per kilogram of ideal body weight, not exceeding 10-20% of our total daily calorie intake. Proteins can have either animal or plant origins. Animal sources include eggs, milk and its derivatives, fish, and meat, while plant-based sources include soy, rice, legumes, and cereals. Ideally, one-third of protein intake should be from animal sources, and two-thirds from plant sources.

Sugars and sweeteners

Guidelines set by the World Health Organization (WHO) recommend daily intake of simple sugars to be below 10% of the total daily energy intake. This recommendation is even more crucial for individuals with diabetes. It's important to note that this recommendation excludes naturally occurring sugars in fresh fruits and vegetables or in milk, focusing on sugars added to foods and beverages, as well as those naturally present in honey and fruit juices produced from concentrates.

As a result, products labeled "sugar-free" and artificially sweetened are increasingly prevalent in the market. Artificial sweeteners have significantly lower caloric value than sugar, but it would be incorrect to consider them biologically inert; they can indeed alter glycemic and insulin responses. Enhancing the sweet taste also predisposes the body to expect additional calories, leading to altered signals of hunger and satiety. Thus, it is not accurate to assume that "sugar-free" products can be consumed freely.Choosing a product rich in fiber and with few natural sugars is always a better option than a product with fewer fibers and artificial sweeteners. Remember that fibers are crucial for modulating the glycemic response to a meal. Common sweeteners include cyclamate, aspartame, saccharin, mannitol, sorbitol, xylitol, and stevia.

Pay attention to fructose; while it has a low glycemic index, its metabolic consequences are concerning. Fructose, despite being a sugar, is metabolized as fat and raises blood triglyceride levels. Therefore, it's advisable to avoid foods where fructose is artificially added as a sweetener. Finally, it's worth noting that there hasn't been demonstrated a specific advantage in consuming "diabetic-friendly" foods. In reality, these products often cost more than regular alternatives without providing significant benefits.

Spices

Incorporating certain spices into the diet can help lower the glycemic index of food:

- Cinnamon
- Cloves
- Turmeric
- Curry
- Ginger
- Allspice
- Bay leaves

CHAPTER 2: BREAKFAST

Quinoa breakfast bowl with almonds and raspberries

Ingredients for 2 people:
- 100 g quinoa (3.5 oz)
- 240 ml water (1 cup)
- 60 ml unsweetened almond milk (¼ cup)
- 50 g fresh raspberries (1.75 oz)
- 20 g sliced almonds (0.7 oz)
- 1 tsp vanilla extract
- 1 tsp cinnamon

Preparation:
1. Rinse the quinoa under cold water.
2. In a saucepan, combine quinoa and water. Bring to a boil, then reduce heat and simmer for 15 minutes or until quinoa is cooked and water is absorbed.
3. Stir in the almond milk, vanilla extract, and cinnamon. Cook for another 2 minutes.
4. Divide the quinoa mixture into two bowls.
5. Top each bowl with half the raspberries and half the sliced almonds.

Nutritional values: Calories: 250 Kcal , Carbohydrates: 35 g, Lipid: 8 g, Proteins: 8 g

Greek yogurt with berries and nuts

Ingredients for 2 people:
- 200 g Greek yogurt (7 oz)
- 100 g mixed berries (3.5 oz)
- 20 g chopped nuts (0.7 oz)
- 1 tsp honey (optional)

Preparation:
1. Divide the yogurt equally into two bowls.
2. Top each bowl with half the berries and half the nuts.
3. Drizzle with honey if desired.

Nutritional values: Calories: 180 kcal, Carbohydrates: 15 g, Lipid: 9 g, Proteins: 10 g

Oatmeal with apple and cinnamon

Ingredients for 2 people:

- 80 g rolled oats (3 oz)
- 240 ml water or unsweetened almond milk (1 cup)
- 1 medium apple, chopped
- 1 tsp ground cinnamon
- 1 tsp chia seeds

Preparation:

1. Cook the oats with water or almond milk as per package instructions.
2. Stir in the chopped apple and cinnamon.
3. Sprinkle with chia seeds before serving.

Nutritional values: Calories: 190 Kcal , Carbohydrates: 32 g, Lipid: 3 g, Proteins: 5 g

Chia seed pudding with vanilla and berries

Ingredients for 2 people:

- 60 g chia seeds (2 oz)
- 480 ml unsweetened almond milk (2 cups)
- 1 tsp vanilla extract
- 100 g mixed berries (3.5 oz)

Preparation:

1. Combine chia seeds, almond milk, and vanilla extract in a bowl.
2. Stir well and refrigerate for at least 2 hours or overnight.
3. Serve topped with mixed berries.

Nutritional values: Calories: 220 kcal, Carbohydrates: 12 g, Lipid: 14 g, Proteins: 6 g

Cottage cheese with pineapple and flaxseeds

Ingredients for 2 people:
- 200 g cottage cheese (7 oz)
- 100 g fresh pineapple, chopped (3.5 oz)
- 2 tsp flaxseeds

Preparation:
1. Divide cottage cheese equally into two bowls.
2. Top with pineapple and flaxseeds.

Nutritional values: Calories: 160 Kcal , Carbohydrates: 10 g, Lipid: 6 g, Proteins: 15 g

Almond flour pancakes with blueberries

Ingredients for 2 people:
- 60 g almond flour (2 oz)
- 2 eggs
- 1 tsp baking powder
- 60 ml unsweetened almond milk (¼ cup)
- 100 g blueberries (3.5 oz)

Preparation:
1. Mix almond flour, eggs, baking powder, and almond milk in a bowl.
2. Cook small pancakes on a non-stick skillet.
3. Serve with blueberries on top.

Nutritional values: Calories: 210 Kcal , Carbohydrates: 12 g, Lipid: 15 g, Proteins: 10 g

Smoothie with spinach, banana, and peanut butter

Ingredients for 2 people:
- 1 banana
- 60 g fresh spinach (2 oz)
- 240 ml unsweetened almond milk (1 cup)
- 2 tbsp peanut butter

Preparation:
1. Blend all ingredients until smooth.
2. Divide into two glasses and serve.

Nutritional values: Calories: 220 Kcal , Carbohydrates: 25 g, Lipid: 12 g, Proteins: 6 g

Whole wheat toast with avocado and strawberry

Ingredients for 2 people:
- 2 slices whole wheat bread
- 1 avocado
- 100 g strawberries, sliced (3.5 oz)

Preparation:
1. Toast the bread.
2. Mash the avocado and spread it on the toast.
3. Top with sliced strawberries.

Nutritional values: Calories: 220 Kcal , Carbohydrates: 25 g, Lipid: 13 g, Proteins: 5 g

Ciambellone (italian ring cake)

Ingredients for 2 people:
- 1 Egg
- 1 Egg Yolk
- 25ml Whole Milk
- 150g All-Purpose Flour (Type 00) -> Approximately 1.06 cups
- 37.5g Sugar -> Approximately 3 tablespoons
- 35ml Vegetable Oil
- A pinch of Salt
- 1/4 packet Baking Powder for Sweets
- Zest of one Lemon

Preparation:
1. Preheat the oven to 180°C (356°F).
2. In a bowl, break the eggs and mix them with sugar and a pinch of salt.
3. Add lemon zest, vegetable oil, and milk gradually while continuously stirring.
4. Finally, add sifted flour and baking powder, mixing well.
5. Grease and flour a ring-shaped cake mold and pour the batter into it.
6. Bake the cake in the preheated oven at 180°C (356°F) for 35-40 minutes.
7. Perform the toothpick test: if it comes out clean, the ciambellone is ready; otherwise, bake for a few more minutes.
8. Allow the ciambellone to cool thoroughly before removing it from the mold to prevent it from breaking.

Nutritional values: Calories: about 260 Kcal, Carbohydrates:about 40 g, Lipid: about 10 g, Proteins: about 5,6 g

Cocoa and raspberry pancakes

Ingredients for 2 people:
- 60g Whole Wheat Flour -> Approximately 1/2 cup
- 65g Semi-Skimmed Milk -> Approximately 1/4 cup
- 25g Whole Cane Sugar -> Approximately 2 tablespoons
- 1 Egg
- A pinch of Salt
- 1 teaspoon Baking Powder
- 1 teaspoon Unsweetened Cocoa Powder (about 4-5g)
- 100g Raspberries

Preparation:
1. In a bowl, combine all the ingredients and knead for a few minutes until the mixture becomes smooth and free of lumps.
2. Perform the spoon test: the batter should have the right consistency when it easily slides off the spoon (add a few drops of milk if it thickens too much).
3. Once you have obtained this liquid batter, let it rest in the refrigerator for 5-10 minutes.
4. Heat a flat non-stick pan, take the batter, mix with a spoon, and using a ladle, pour the content onto the pan to form small discs.
5. When bubbles form, flip the pancake and let it cook for about 20 seconds over medium heat.
6. Garnish with raspberries towards the end of cooking.

Nutritional values: Calories: about 210 Kcal , Carbohydrates: about 22 g, Lipid: about 5 g, Proteins: about 8 g

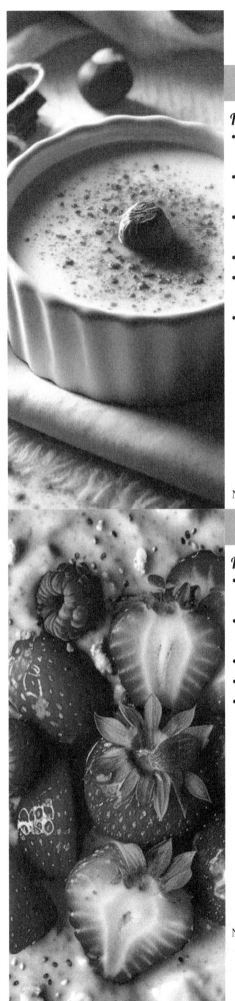

Baked sweet milk

Ingredients for 2 people:

- 500ml Semi-Skimmed Milk -> Approximately 2 cups
- 50g All-Purpose Flour -> Approximately 1/3 cup
- 17.5g Stevia Powder -> Approximately 4 teaspoons
- Two Eggs (about 120g)
- Grated Peel of an untreated Lemon
- Ground Cinnamon or Hazelnut Granules (to taste)

Preparation:

1. Boil semi-skimmed milk.
2. Sift 50g (1,76 ounces) of all-purpose flour to avoid the formation of lumps.
3. Dissolve 50g (1,76 ounces) of all-purpose flour in a small amount of milk. Add 17.5g (0,61 ounces) of Stevia.
4. Grate the peel of one untreated lemon. Add the 4 eggs, previously beaten.
5. Mix everything thoroughly.
6. Cook over medium heat, stirring until the mixture thickens, trying not to let it stick to the bottom of the pot.
7. After cooking, transfer the mixture into individual dessert cups and let the sweet milk cool before serving.
8. Garnish as desired with cinnamon or hazelnut granules.

Nutritional values: Calories: about 215 Kcal , Carbohydrates: about 27 g, Lipid: about 6 g, Proteins: about 12 g

Vanilla yogurt and strawberry pudding

Ingredients for 2 people:

- Low-fat Yogurt: 100g -> Approximately 3.5 ounces
- Ripe Strawberries: 150g -> Approximately 5.3 ounces
- Sweetener: 1 packet
- Vanilla Extract: 1 drop
- Gelatin Sheets: 1/2 packet

Preparation:

1. Clean and wash the strawberries. Gently pat them dry to remove excess water, then cut them into small pieces and sweeten with the sweetener. Add vanilla extract and blend.
2. Mix the yogurt into the strawberry blend and stir well.
3. In a separate bowl, soak the gelatin sheets in cold water, dissolve them in two tablespoons of very hot water, and gently incorporate them into the mixture.
4. Pour the mixture into individual molds and let it cool in the refrigerator for at least two hours.
5. Unmold and serve.

Nutritional values: Calories: about 55 Kcal , Carbohydrates: about 19 g, Lipid: about 1 g, Proteins: about 3 g

CHAPTER 3: FIRST DISHES

Quinoa-stuffed bell peppers

Ingredients for 2 people:
- 2 large bell peppers (red, yellow, or green)
- 1/2 cup quinoa
- 1 cup low-sodium vegetable broth
- 1/4 cup diced tomatoes (canned, no added sugar)
- 1/4 cup diced zucchini
- 1/4 cup diced mushrooms
- 1/4 cup diced onions
- 1 clove garlic, minced
- 1 tablespoon olive oil
- Salt and pepper to taste
- Fresh herbs (such as parsley or basil) for garnish

Preparation:
1. Preheat the oven to 375°F (190°C).
2. Cut the tops off the bell peppers and remove the seeds and membranes. Place the peppers in a baking dish, cut side up.
3. Rinse the quinoa under cold water. In a saucepan, combine the quinoa and vegetable broth. Bring to a boil, then reduce the heat to low, cover, and simmer for 15-20 minutes, or until the quinoa is cooked and the liquid is absorbed.
4. In a skillet, heat the olive oil over medium heat. Add the onions and garlic and sauté until softened, about 3-4 minutes.
5. Add the diced tomatoes, zucchini, and mushrooms to the skillet. Cook for another 5 minutes, or until the vegetables are tender.
6. Stir the cooked quinoa into the skillet with the vegetables. Season with salt and pepper to taste.
7. Spoon the quinoa mixture into the bell peppers, packing it tightly. Replace the tops of the peppers.
8. Cover the baking dish with aluminum foil and bake in the preheated oven for 25-30 minutes, or until the peppers are tender.
9. Remove the foil and bake for an additional 5 minutes to lightly brown the tops of the peppers.
10. Serve the stuffed peppers garnished with fresh herbs.

Nutritional values: Calories: 220 kcal, Carbohydrates: 35 grams, Lipid: 6 grams, Proteins: 7 grams

Pasta and cauliflower minestrone

Ingredients for 2 people:
- Cauliflower: 500g -> Cauliflower: about 17.6 ounces
- Extra virgin olive oil: 25g -> Extra virgin olive oil: about 1.76 tablespoons
- Garlic: 1 clove -> Garlic: 1 clove
- Peeled tomatoes: 2 or 3 (or Tomato paste: 1 tablespoon) -> Peeled tomatoes: 2 or 3 (or Tomato paste: 1 tablespoon)
- Chopped parsley: 1/4 tablespoon -> Chopped parsley: 1/4 tablespoon
- Laganelle (small fettuccine) in pieces: 150g -> Laganelle (small fettuccine) in pieces: about 5.3 ounces
- Salt, red pepper -> Salt, red pepper

Preparation:
1. Sauté the garlic with the olive oil. Remove the cores from the cauliflower and cut it into pieces. Put it in the pot with the peeled tomatoes (or tomato paste), red pepper, and a couple of ladles of water. Cover the pot, and stirring occasionally, cook the cauliflower until it is tender.
2. In a separate pot, boil the pasta in salted water. After draining it, add it to the cauliflower.
3. Let it rest for 5 or 10 minutes and serve it hot.

Nutritional values: Calories: about 442 Kcal , Carbohydrates: about 35 g, Lipid: about 13,3 g, Proteins: about 13 g

Zucchini noodles with pesto and cherry tomatoes

Ingredients for 2 people:
- 2 medium zucchinis (about 400 g total) (14 oz)
- 100 g cherry tomatoes, halved (3.5 oz)
- 2 tbsp pesto sauce
- 2 tbsp pine nuts
- 1 tbsp olive oil
- 2 tbsp grated Parmesan cheese
- Salt and pepper to taste

Preparation:
1. Spiralize the zucchinis into noodles.
2. Heat olive oil in a large pan over medium heat.
3. Add zucchini noodles and cook for 3-4 minutes until tender.
4. Stir in the pesto sauce and cherry tomatoes.
5. Cook for another 2 minutes until heated through.
6. Divide into two bowls and top with pine nuts and Parmesan cheese.
7. Season with salt and pepper to taste.

Nutritional values: Calories: 300 Kcal , Carbohydrates: 10 g, Lipid: 26 g, Proteins: 8 g

Buckwheat pasta with roasted vegetables

Ingredients for 2 people:
- 100g buckwheat pasta (dry weight) (3.5 oz)
- 100g red bell peppers, diced (1 cup)
- 100g zucchini, diced (1 cup)
- 100g eggplant, diced (1 cup)
- 15ml olive oil (1 tablespoon)
- 1 clove garlic, minced
- Salt and pepper to taste
- 10g fresh parsley, chopped (1 tablespoon)

Preparation:
1. Preheat the oven to 200°C (400°F). Place the red bell peppers, zucchini, and eggplant on a baking sheet. Drizzle with olive oil, season with salt and pepper. Roast for 25-30 minutes, or until the vegetables are tender and slightly caramelized.
2. Cook the buckwheat pasta according to the package instructions.
3. In a large skillet, sauté the minced garlic with a drizzle of olive oil until golden.
4. Add the roasted vegetables and cooked pasta to the skillet with garlic. Mix well to combine all the ingredients.
5. Garnish with chopped fresh parsley before serving.

Nutritional values: Calories: 300 kcal, Carbohydrates: 45g, Lipid: 8g, Proteins: 10g

Whole wheat spaghetti with tomato and spinach

Ingredients for 2 people:
- 100g whole wheat spaghetti (dry weight) (3.5 oz)
- 150g cherry tomatoes, halved (1 cup)
- 60g fresh spinach (2 cups)
- 2 cloves garlic, minced
- 15ml olive oil (1 tbsp)
- Salt and pepper to taste

Preparation:
1. Cook spaghetti according to package instructions.
2. Sauté garlic in olive oil, add tomatoes and cook until soft.
3. Add spinach and cook until wilted.
4. Toss cooked pasta with tomato-spinach mixture.

Nutritional values: Calories: 340 kcal, Carbohydrates: 42g, Lipids: 6g, Proteins: 11g

Chickpea pasta with lemon and broccoli

Ingredients for 2 people:
- 100g chickpea pasta (dry weight) (3.5 oz)
- 150g broccoli florets (1 cup)
- 1 lemon, zest and juice
- 15ml olive oil (1 tbsp)
- 1 clove garlic, minced
- Salt and pepper to taste

Preparation:
1. Cook pasta according to package instructions.
2. Steam broccoli until tender.
3. Sauté garlic in olive oil, add lemon zest and juice.
4. Toss pasta and broccoli with lemon mixture.

Nutritional values: Calories: 260 kcal, Carbohydrates: 30g, Lipids: 5g, Proteins: 14g

Lentil pasta with tomato basil sauce

Ingredients for 2 people:
- 100g lentil pasta (dry weight) (3.5 oz)
- 240g canned diced tomatoes (1 cup)
- 15g fresh basil leaves (1/2 cup)
- 15ml olive oil (1 tbsp)
- 2 cloves garlic, minced
- Salt and pepper to taste

Preparation:
1. Cook pasta according to package instructions.
2. Sauté garlic in olive oil, add tomatoes and simmer for 10 minutes.
3. Stir in basil leaves and cook for another 2 minutes.
4. Toss pasta with tomato basil sauce.

Nutritional values: Calories: 290 kcal, Carbohydrates: 35g, Lipids: 4g, Proteins: 18g

Cauliflower alfredo with whole wheat fettuccine

Ingredients for 2 people:
- 100g whole wheat fettuccine (dry weight) (3.5 oz)
- 100g cauliflower florets (1 cup)
- 120ml unsweetened almond milk (1/2 cup)
- 25g grated Parmesan cheese (1/4 cup)
- 1 clove garlic, minced
- 15ml olive oil (1 tbsp)
- Salt and pepper to taste

Preparation:
1. Cook pasta according to package instructions.
2. Steam cauliflower until tender and blend with almond milk, garlic, Parmesan, and olive oil until smooth.
3. Toss pasta with cauliflower Alfredo sauce.

Nutritional values: Calories: 350 kcal, Carbohydrates: 45g, Lipids: 6g, Proteins: 15g

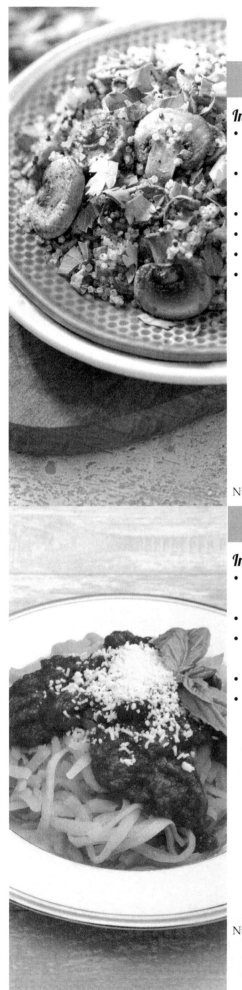

Quinoa pasta with mushrooms and kale

Ingredients for 2 people:
- 100g quinoa pasta (dry weight) (3.5 oz)
- 100g mushrooms, sliced (1 cup)
- 60g kale, chopped (2 cups)
- 15ml olive oil (1 tbsp)
- 2 cloves garlic, minced
- Salt and pepper to taste

Preparation:
1. Cook pasta according to package instructions.
2. Sauté garlic in olive oil, add mushrooms and cook until tender.
3. Add kale and cook until wilted.
4. Toss pasta with mushroom and kale mixture.

Nutritional values: Calories: 310 kcal, Carbohydrates: 40g, Lipids: 5g, Proteins: 13g

Spaghetti squash with marinara

Ingredients for 2 people:
- 900g spaghetti squash (1 medium squash)
- 240g marinara sauce (1 cup)
- 25g grated Parmesan cheese (1/4 cup)
- 15ml olive oil (1 tbsp)
- Salt and pepper to taste

Preparation:
1. Cut squash in half, remove seeds, and bake at 200°C (400°F) for 40 minutes.
2. Scrape out the strands with a fork.
3. Heat marinara sauce, mix with squash strands, and top with Parmesan cheese.

Nutritional values: Calories: 200 kcal, Carbohydrates: 18g, Lipids: 7g, Proteins: 7g

Brown rice pasta with peas and mint

Ingredients for 2 people:
- 100g brown rice pasta (dry weight) (3.5 oz)
- 150g frozen peas (1 cup)
- 10g fresh mint leaves (1/4 cup)
- 15ml olive oil (1 tbsp)
- 1 clove garlic, minced
- Salt and pepper to taste

Preparation:
1. Cook pasta according to package instructions.
2. Steam peas until tender.
3. Sauté garlic in olive oil, add peas and mint.
4. Toss pasta with pea and mint mixture.

Nutritional values: Calories: 350, Carbohydrates: 45g, Lipids: 4g, Proteins: 10g

Spelt pasta with artichokes and lemon

Ingredients for 2 people:
- 100g spelt pasta (dry weight) (3.5 oz)
- 150g canned artichoke hearts, drained and chopped (1 cup)
- 1 lemon, zest and juice
- 15ml olive oil (1 tbsp)
- 1 clove garlic, minced
- Salt and pepper to taste

Preparation:
1. Cook pasta according to package instructions.
2. Sauté garlic in olive oil, add artichokes and cook until heated through.
3. Add lemon zest and juice.
4. Toss pasta with artichoke lemon mixture.

Nutritional values: Calories: 320 kcal, Carbohydrates: 40g, Lipids: 5g, Proteins: 11g

Black bean pasta with avocado and lime

Ingredients for 2 people:

- 100g black bean pasta (dry weight) (3.5 oz)
- 150g avocado, diced (1 avocado)
- 1 lime, zest and juice
- 15ml olive oil (1 tbsp)
- Salt and pepper to taste

Preparation:

1. Cook pasta according to package instructions.
2. Toss pasta with avocado, lime zest and juice, and olive oil.
3. Season with salt and pepper to taste.

Nutritional values: Calories: 350 kcal, Carbohydrates: 30g, Lipids: 14g, Proteins: 18g

Artichokes in rice salad

Ingredients for 2 people:

- Rice: 250g -> Rice: about 8.8 ounces
- Butter (unsalted): 25g -> Butter (unsalted): about 1.8 tablespoons
- Lemon: 1/2
- Onions: 1
- Tomatoes: 4
- Garlic cloves: 2
- Pitted black olives: 10
- Artichoke hearts: 4
- Lettuce/Chicory: 1/2
- Parsley: as needed
- Black Pepper: as needed

Preparation:

1. Boil salted water and cook the rice.
2. Add butter and let it cream in a covered pot for 15-30 minutes. Let the rice cool.
3. Mix together lemon juice, crushed garlic, chopped onions, olives, parsley, 1 teaspoon of salt, black pepper, and diced tomatoes.
4. Add the mixture to the cooled rice and mix. Let it rest in the pot for a good period (from 30 minutes to 3 hours).
5. Marinate the artichoke hearts and finally assemble the dish with the rice served on a bed of lettuce or chicory with the artichokes.

Nutritional values: Calories: about 200 Kcal , Carbohydrates: about 36 g, Lipid: about 5 g, Proteins: about 5 g

Baked tagliatelle with ricotta

Ingredients for 2 people:

- 250g Spinach -> Spinach: about 8.8 ounces
- 100g Cow's Milk Ricotta -> Cow's Milk Ricotta: about 3.5 ounces
- 10g Butter -> Butter: about 0.35 ounces (approximately 2 teaspoons)
- 160g Tagliatelle -> Tagliatelle: about 5.6 ounces
- 10g Grated Parmesan -> Grated Parmesan: about 0.35 ounces

Preparation:

1. Clean the spinach, wash them, and cook them in very little water. Squeeze them and finely chop, then sauté them in butter.
2. Boil the tagliatelle al dente, drain them while keeping them slightly moist, and place them in an ovenproof dish.
3. Season the tagliatelle with spinach, ricotta, and finally, the Parmesan.
4. Bake for approximately 15 minutes in a preheated oven at 200°C (392 °F).

For those who prefer not to use the oven, simply toss the tagliatelle with spinach and ricotta. When serving, sprinkle with Grana cheese and a dash of nutmeg. The key to the success of this pasta is the ricotta, which should be very fresh.

Nutritional values: Calories: about 470 Kcal , Carbohydrates: about 45 g, Lipid: about 14 g, Proteins: about 24 g

Lemon penne

Ingredients for 2 people:

- Lemon Zest: 1/2 teaspoon
- Rigatoni Pasta: 125g -> about 4.4 ounces
- Chives: 1/2 tablespoon
- Olive Oil: 1 tablespoon
- Fresh Thyme Leaves: 1 tablespoon
- Salt, Pepper, and Parmesan Cheese

Preparation:

1. Bring a pot of moderately salted water to a boil and cook the pasta according to the instructions on the box.
2. Add the cheese, thyme, oil, chives, and lemon zest; sprinkle and mix.
3. Adjust the taste with salt and pepper.
4. Serve immediately with optional Parmesan cheese.

Nutritional values: Calories: about 267 Kcal , Carbohydrates: about 47 g, Lipid: about 6 g, Proteins: about 12 g

Spelt salad with peppers and zucchini

Ingredients for 2 people:
- 100 grams of whole spelt -> about 3.5 ounces
- 1 bell pepper
- 1 medium-sized zucchini
- 1 tablespoon of sesame seeds
- 1 clove of garlic
- 1 tablespoon of extra virgin olive oil
- 1/2 teaspoon of parsley
- 2 bay leaves
- 6 basil leaves
- Oregano to taste

Preparation:
1. Cook the spelt in boiling salted water according to the instructions on the package.
2. Clean and dice the bell pepper and zucchini. In a pan greased with 1 tablespoon of oil, sauté the bell peppers with garlic, bay leaves, and sesame seeds. Cover and cook for 5 minutes, adding a splash of water if necessary.
3. Then, add the zucchini and cook for another 5 minutes.
4. Incorporate the cooked spelt, chopped parsley, chopped basil, oregano, and mix well.
5. Serve warm or cold.

Nutritional values: Calories: about 350 Kcal , Carbohydrates: about 50 g, Lipid: about 10 g, Proteins: about 10 g

Spaghetti with fresh clams

Ingredients for 2 people:
- 140 g spaghetti -> about 5 ounces
- 1.5 tablespoons extra virgin olive oil
- 500 g fresh clams -> about 17.6 ounces
- 1 clove of garlic
- Quarter glass of white wine
- Chopped parsley to taste
- Salt to taste
- Red chili flakes to taste

Preparation:
1. Rinse the clams thoroughly and let them purge in a bowl of water with coarse salt for at least 2-3 hours.
2. In a wide, shallow pan, heat the olive oil, garlic, and chili flakes.
3. Drain the clams well, rinse them, and pour them into the hot pan. Cover with a lid, let them cook for a few minutes over high heat, and shake the pan occasionally until the clams are completely open.
4. Pour half a glass of white wine and let it evaporate. Shell half of the clams and leave them in the sauce; set aside the other half.
5. Bring a pot of water to boil for the spaghetti. Cook them al dente, drain, and toss them in the pan with the shelled clams, mixing well and adding chopped parsley.
6. Plate the dish, adding the unshelled clams on top.

Nutritional values: Calories: about 350 Kcal , Carbohydrates: about 45 g, Lipid: about 9 g, Proteins: about 20 g

Spaghetti with anchovies sauce

Ingredients for 2 people:

- 233 g anchovies (already gutted) -> about 8.2 ounces
- 167 g spaghetti -> about 5.9 ounces
- 1 small onion
- 1 garlic clove
- 267 g canned tomatoes -> about 9.4 ounces
- White wine to taste
- Extra virgin olive oil
- Salt to taste
- Parsley
- Red pepper flakes

Preparation:

1. Sauté the finely chopped onion and garlic in olive oil over low heat, then add the anchovy mixture along with white wine, parsley, and red pepper flakes.
2. Cook for 20 minutes, ensuring it doesn't stick.
3. Add the canned tomatoes and cook for an additional 15 minutes.
4. Season the spaghetti with the anchovy mixture, adding freshly chopped parsley.

Nutritional values: Calories: about 500 Kcal , Carbohydrates: about 50 g, Lipid: about 20 g, Proteins: about 25 g

Spaghetti with cob sauce

Ingredients for 2 people:

- 333 g mantis shrimp (sea cicadas) -> about 11.7 ounces
- 167 g spaghetti -> about 5.9 ounces
- 167 g tomato pulp -> about 5.9 ounces
- 1 onion
- Extra virgin olive oil
- Chopped parsley
- Salt to taste

Preparation:

1. Sauté the finely chopped onion in olive oil. Once it starts to color, add the mantis shrimp cut into 2-3 pieces.
2. Let it cook for a few minutes, then add the tomato pulp, salt, and parsley. Finish cooking.
3. Season the spaghetti, freshly drained al dente, with the sauce and fresh parsley.

Nutritional values: Calories: about 400 Kcal , Carbohydrates: about 50 g, Lipid: about 8 g, Proteins: about 30 g

Riso venere with cherry tomatoes and shrimp

Ingredients for 2 people:

- 150 g Black Venus rice -> about 5.3 ounces
- 100 g cherry tomatoes -> about 3.5 ounces
- 200 g shrimp -> about 7 ounces
- Chives
- Half a lemon
- 1 tablespoon extra virgin olive oil

Preparation:

1. Rinse the Black Venus rice under running water and cook it in plenty of salted water for about 40 minutes. Drain it al dente and run it under cold water to stop the cooking process.
2. Meanwhile, cook the shrimp, flavoring them with the juice of half a lemon, and cut the cherry tomatoes into cubes.
3. Once cooked, combine all the ingredients, dress with 1 tablespoon of raw extra virgin olive oil, and garnish with chives.
4. This recipe is also excellent to be enjoyed cold.

Nutritional values: Calories: about 200 Kcal , Carbohydrates: about 31 g, Lipid: about 4 g, Proteins: about 10

Green gnocchetti

Ingredients for 2 people:

- Fresh Spinach: 200g -> about 7 ounces
- Flour: 100g -> about 3.5 ounces
- Egg: 1
- Whole Milk: 100ml -> about 3.4 fluid ounces
- Butter: 10g -> about 0.35 ounces
- Prosciutto Crudo (raw ham): 50g -> about 1.75 ounces
- Prosciutto Cotto (cooked ham): 25g -> about 0.9 ounces
- Salt: to taste

Preparation:

1. Cook the spinach thoroughly, then squeeze them, blend them, and mix with flour, milk, and egg until the mixture is thick. Add more milk or flour if necessary.
2. Meanwhile, bring water to a boil, adding salt. Once it boils, immerse the prepared mixture, previously crumbled with a fork or hands, a little at a time. Retrieve them as they float to the surface.
3. Cut both the cooked and raw ham into cubes. Sauté them in a pan with butter and a light stir, then combine the ham with the gnocchetti, ensuring all ingredients are well mixed.

Nutritional values: Calories: about 200 Kcal , Carbohydrates: about 30 g, Lipid: about 13 g, Proteins: about 18 g

Risotto with cuttlefish and mushrooms

Ingredients for 2 people:
- Arborio rice, well cleaned: 150g -> about 5.3 ounces
- Cuttlefish (net weight after cleaning): 80g -> about 2.8 ounces
- Olive oil: 4 teaspoons
- Sliced mushrooms (fresh if possible): 70g -> about 2.5 ounces
- Dry white wine: 2 tablespoons
- A mixture of one clove of garlic and a small piece of onion, finely chopped
- Boiling water
- Salt and pepper

Preparation:
1. Clean the cuttlefish (remove the ink sacs) and wash them thoroughly. Cut them into thin strips.
2. In a saucepan, heat the olive oil and add the finely chopped garlic and onion mixture, along with a pinch of pepper. Once the mixture is golden, add the cuttlefish strips, season with salt, let them flavor for a moment, then pour in the wine diluted with a little water.
3. Cook over moderate heat for about three-quarters of an hour, stirring occasionally. Add the sliced mushrooms and continue cooking over very moderate heat for about ten minutes.
4. When ready to serve, bring the sauce to a boil and add the rice and, if desired, part of the ink from the ink sacs to the boiling sauce.
5. As soon as the rice begins to stick to the bottom of the pan, add slightly salted boiling water and complete the cooking by adding more if the rice dries out.
6. Serve al dente and piping hot.

Nutritional values: Calories: about 380 Kcal , Carbohydrates: about 50 g, Lipid: about 15 g, Proteins: about 10 g

Pumpkin soup

Ingredients for 2 people:
- 100 g ridged ditaloni pasta -> about 3.5 ounces
- 300 g pumpkin -> about 10.5 ounces
- 62.5 ml water -> about 1/4 cup + 1 teaspoon
- 300 ml whole milk -> about 1 1/4 cups
- 50 g Grana Padano DOP -> about 1.75 ounces
- Salt to taste
- Black pepper to taste

Preparation:
1. Cut the pumpkin into wedges, clean it from seeds and internal filaments, and remove the skin. Cut it into 1-2 cm thick pieces and place it in a pot.
2. Add water, adjust salt and pepper, then stew the pumpkin for a few minutes, covering the pot with a lid. Once cooked, blend it with a mixer until you get a smooth cream.
3. In another pot, bring the milk to a boil. Then add the pumpkin, stirring carefully.
4. Pour the pasta into the obtained velvety mixture and let it cook over moderate heat, stirring frequently to prevent it from sticking to the bottom.
5. Finally, add the grated Grana Padano, reserving some for plating. Optionally, you can add a sprinkle of freshly grated nutmeg or chopped rosemary.

Nutritional values: Calories: about 350 Kcal , Carbohydrates: about 50 g, Lipid: about 10 g, Proteins: about 15 g

CHAPTER 4: SOUPS

Black cabbage and cannellini bean soup

Ingredients for 2 people:
- 100 g dried cannellini beans or 300 g cooked -> 3.5 ounces dried cannellini beans or about 10.5 ounces cooked
- 0.5 small bunch of black cabbage
- 0.5 clove of garlic
- 0.5 onion
- Sage leaves to taste
- 1/2 cup vegetable broth (prepared by boiling 1 celery stalk, 1 carrot, and 1 onion for 30 minutes) -> 120 ml vegetable broth
- Iodized salt to taste
- Pepper to taste
- 4 slices of toasted rye bread. In the case of gluten intolerance, use gluten-free bread.

Preparation:
1. Soak the beans overnight and then cook them in a pressure cooker with 1 garlic clove, a few sage leaves, and a piece of kombu seaweed.
2. Meanwhile, clean the black cabbage, removing all the stems, and sauté it with extra virgin olive oil, finely chopped onion, and garlic, gradually adding the vegetable broth.
3. When the cabbage is cooked, add the beans and season with plenty of iodized salt and pepper.
4. Serve with 4 slices of toasted rye bread or gluten-free bread.

Nutritional values: Calories: about 250 Kcal , Carbohydrates: about 45 g, Lipid: about 2 g, Proteins: about 15 g

Chickpea and leek soup

Ingredients for 2 people:
- 100 g dried chickpeas (or 300 g precooked) -> 3.5 ounces dried chickpeas (or about 10.5 ounces precooked)
- 125 g leeks, finely chopped -> 4.4 ounces leeks, finely chopped
- Mixture of chopped carrots, celery, and onions
- 10 g extra virgin olive oil -> 2 teaspoons extra virgin olive oil
- 300 ml water or vegetable broth (prepared by boiling 1 celery stalk, 1 carrot, and 1 onion for 30 minutes) -> 1.27 cups water or vegetable broth
- 2 slices of toasted whole-grain bread. In case of gluten intolerance, use gluten-free bread.

Preparation:
1. Soak the chickpeas in plenty of water for 24 hours, then cook them until al dente. The cooking time depends on the type of chickpeas and the pot used. Set them aside.
2. In a pot, heat the olive oil and sauté the finely chopped leeks until tender. Add a little water and let it simmer for 5 minutes.
3. Add the cooked chickpeas and their cooking water along with the vegetable broth. Continue cooking for 15 minutes.
4. Blend the soup with a mixer until smooth. Serve the hot soup with toasted whole-grain or gluten-free bread.

Nutritional values: Calories: about 200 Kcal , Carbohydrates: about 35 g, Lipid: about 5 g, Proteins: about 8 g

Lentil soup

Ingredients for 2 people:
- 100 g Castelluccio lentils -> 3.5 ounces Castelluccio lentils
- 100 g ripe cherry tomatoes -> 3.5 ounces ripe cherry tomatoes
- 1/2 onion
- 1/2 medium carrot
- 1/2 celery stalk
- 1 bay leaf
- 1 small hot chili pepper (optional, to taste)
- Iodized salt to taste
- 1/2 garlic clove
- 1.5 tablespoons extra virgin olive oil
- 2 slices of toasted whole-grain bread. In case of gluten intolerance, use gluten-free bread.

Preparation:
1. Rinse the lentils thoroughly.
2. Thinly slice the onion, carrot, and celery.
3. In a pot, combine the lentils, bay leaf, optional chili pepper, onion, carrot, celery, and cherry tomatoes. Add 1 liter of water (or vegetable broth) and bring to a boil.
4. Cook over low heat with a lid for 45 minutes from the beginning of boiling.
5. At the end of cooking, remove the bay leaf and chili pepper. Season with salt, and if needed, add a little water or broth to adjust the soup's density.
6. Serve with toasted whole-grain bread (or gluten-free bread) and drizzle each serving with 1 teaspoon of extra virgin olive oil.

Nutritional values: Calories: about 280 Kcal , Carbohydrates: about 30 g, Lipid: about 5 g, Proteins: about 8 g

Borlotti bean soup

Ingredients for 2 people:
- 150 g shelled fresh borlotti beans -> 5.3 ounces shelled fresh borlotti beans
- 1/2 medium onion
- 1/2 medium leek
- 1 clove of garlic
- 50 g celeriac -> 1.8 ounces celeriac
- 2 tablespoons extra virgin olive oil
- 2 tablespoons mixed rosemary, sage, bay leaves
- Salt in moderation
- Pepper
- 1 tablespoon Grana Padano cheese, grated

Preparation:
1. After soaking the beans, wash and chop the vegetables.
2. In a non-stick pot, add 1 tablespoon of oil, chopped vegetables, and the clove of garlic. Sauté for about 5 minutes.
3. Add the drained and rinsed beans, cover with water twice the volume of the beans in the pot, season with salt and pepper.
4. Cook over low heat for 2 and a half hours, and if necessary, add water to adjust the consistency.
5. At the end of cooking, blend the soup, reserving 3-4 tablespoons of whole beans, which will be added before serving.
6. In a small saucepan with the remaining oil, heat the aromatic herbs without frying. Turn off the heat and let it cool. Strain the flavored oil with a sieve and add it to the bean puree.
7. Pasta, especially "maltagliati," can be added to this soup. Sprinkle a tablespoon of grated Grana Padano on top.
8. Serve hot.

Nutritional values: Calories: about 250 Kcal , Carbohydrates: about 30 g, Lipid: about 12 g, Proteins: about 7 g

Lentil and vegetable soup

Ingredients for 2 people:

- 120 g dry lentils (4.2 oz)
- 1 medium carrot, diced
- 1 celery stalk, diced
- 1 small onion, chopped
- 2 garlic cloves, minced
- 400 ml vegetable broth (1 2/3 cups)
- 1 tbsp olive oil
- 1 tsp ground cumin
- 1 tsp dried thyme
- Salt and pepper to taste

Preparation:

1. Rinse the lentils under cold water.
2. In a large pot, heat olive oil over medium heat.
3. Add the onion, garlic, carrot, and celery. Sauté until vegetables are softened, about 5 minutes.
4. Add lentils, vegetable broth, cumin, and thyme.
5. Bring to a boil, then reduce heat and simmer for about 25-30 minutes until lentils are tender.
6. Season with salt and pepper to taste.
7. Divide the soup into two bowls and serve.

Nutritional values: Calories: 250 Kcal , Carbohydrates: 38 g, Lipid: 6 g, Proteins: 12 g

Bean and cabbage soup

Ingredients for 2 people:

- 150 g Tuscan kale -> 5.3 ounces Tuscan kale
- 150 g ripe tomatoes -> 5.3 ounces ripe tomatoes
- 100 g dried cannellini beans -> 3.5 ounces dried cannellini beans
- 100 g Tuscan bread -> 3.5 ounces Tuscan bread
- 75 g leeks -> 2.6 ounces leeks
- 50 g onion -> 1.8 ounces onion
- 25 g celery -> 0.9 ounces celery
- 10 g extra virgin olive oil -> 0.35 ounces extra virgin olive oil
- 2.5 g garlic -> 0.09 ounces garlic
- 2.5 g dried bay leaves -> 0.09 ounces dried bay leaves
- 0.5 g black pepper -> 0.02 ounces black pepper
- 0.5 g iodized salt -> 0.02 ounces iodized salt

Preparation:

1. Soak the beans in cold water for 12 hours, then rinse them. Put them in a pot with plenty of water and a bay leaf. Cover with a lid, let it boil for 2 hours, and add salt only at the end of cooking.
2. Meanwhile, clean the Tuscan kale and cut it into strips. Blanch the tomatoes, peel, remove the seeds, and chop them. Slice the leeks. Finely chop the onion, garlic, and celery.
3. In a pot with olive oil, combine leeks, onion, garlic, and celery. Sauté for eight minutes.
4. Add the kale and tomatoes; after five minutes, add plenty of bean cooking water and continue cooking for an hour.
5. Add the beans, adjust salt, and turn off the heat after 5 minutes.
6. Toast the slices of bread, place one in each plate, and pour the hot soup over them. Sprinkle generously with pepper, drizzle with the remaining oil, and serve.

Nutritional values: Calories: about 230 Kcal , Carbohydrates: about 35 g, Lipid: about 6 g, Proteins: about 10 g

Mixed cereal and legume soup

Ingredients for 2 people:

- 25 g fregola -> 0.88 ounces fregola
- 10 g lentils -> 0.35 ounces lentils
- 10 g chickpeas -> 0.35 ounces chickpeas
- 10 g quinoa -> 0.35 ounces quinoa
- 10 g barley -> 0.35 ounces barley
- 10 g spelt -> 0.35 ounces spelt
- 15 g onion -> 0.53 ounces onion
- 5 g celery -> 0.18 ounces celery
- 20 g tomato -> 0.71 ounces tomato
- 20 g carrot -> 0.71 ounces carrot
- 0.2 g coriander -> 0.007 ounces coriander
- 0.1 g wild fennel -> 0.0035 ounces wild fennel
- 4 g extra virgin olive oil (1 tablespoon) -> 0.14 ounces extra virgin olive oil
- 0.25 g salt -> 0.009 ounces salt

Vegetable Broth Ingredients:

- 25 g carrots
- 25 g zucchini
- 25 g fennel
- 25 g onion

Preparation:

1. Soak the cereals in cold water for 6 hours. Peel and clean the vegetables (carrots, zucchini, and fennel) and wash them thoroughly under running water.
2. Prepare the vegetable broth by filling a pot with 2 liters (7,57 gallons) of water, adding carrots, zucchini, and fennel, and let it cook for 30 minutes.
3. Drain the water from the previously soaked cereals, rinse them with clean water, and let them drain.
4. Heat the oil in a pot, add the onion, celery, carrot, and then add the drained legumes and cereals. Mix for about a minute and a half.
5. Wash and peel the tomato, cut it into cubes, mix, and let it cook over moderate heat for another 5 minutes.
6. Add the vegetable broth, wild fennel, coriander, slowly bring the soup to a boil, and cook for at least 1 hour.
7. After 1 hour, add the fregola, cook for another 10 minutes, and add more broth if necessary.

Nutritional values: Calories: about 170 Kcal , Carbohydrates: about 32 g, Lipid: about 3 g, Proteins: about 6 g

Minestrone with legumes

Ingredients for 2 people:

- Potatoes: 125 g -> 4.4 ounces potatoes
- Cannellini beans (dry): 15 g -> 0.53 ounces cannellini beans
- Green beans (fresh): 100 g -> 3.5 ounces green beans
- Peas (fresh): 100 g -> 3.5 ounces peas
- Carrots: 60 g (approximately 3 small carrots) -> 2.1 ounces carrots (approximately 3 small carrots)
- Onion: 75 g -> 2.6 ounces onion
- Zucchini: 100 g -> 3.5 ounces zucchini
- Celery stalks: 150 g (approximately 2 stalks) -> 5.3 ounces celery stalks (approximately 2 stalks)
- Spinach: 50 g -> 1.8 ounces spinach
- Genovese Pesto: 10 g -> 0.35 ounces Genovese Pesto
- 1 tablespoon vegetable broth (10 g) -> 1 tablespoon vegetable broth (0.35 ounces)
- Extra virgin olive oil: 20 g -> 0.71 ounces extra virgin olive oil
- Pepper: to taste

Preparation:

1. Cannellini Beans Dry: Soak them in water overnight, then drain and boil for about 1 hour.
2. Green Beans Fresh: Remove the ends and cook them with the other vegetables.
3. Spinach Fresh: Wash them and cook, cut into pieces.
4. Peas Fresh: Remove them from the pod and cook with the other vegetables.
5. Peel and cut potatoes into pieces. Peel carrots and cut them into pieces.
6. Peel onion, clean celery, and zucchini (removing the ends), then cut them into pieces.
7. Put all the chopped vegetables into a large pot, add vegetable broth, and cover with cold water. Cook all the vegetables over medium heat for at least 1 hour and 10 minutes.
8. When all the vegetables are cooked and soft, lightly mash some with a fork, leaving some larger pieces and the rest as a puree.
9. Let the minestrone cool slightly and add Genovese pesto. Mix and add extra virgin olive oil and a little ground pepper (to taste).

Nutritional values: Calories: about 235 Kcal , Carbohydrates: about 36 g, Lipid: about 7 g, Proteins: about 8 g

CHAPTER 5: SECOND DISHES

Ricotta and spinach whole wheat quiche

Ingredients for 2 people:

For the crust:
- 75 g whole wheat flour -> 3/4 cup whole wheat flour
- A pinch of salt
- 35-50 ml lukewarm water -> 2-3 tablespoons lukewarm water
- 35 ml extra virgin olive oil -> 2 1/2 tablespoons extra virgin olive oil

For the filling:
- 1 egg
- 125 g ricotta cheese -> 1/2 cup ricotta cheese
- 250 g spinach -> 8.8 ounces spinach
- 1 tablespoon grated Parmesan cheese
- A handful of pine nuts
- Salt, pepper, nutmeg to taste

Preparation:

1. In a bowl, mix the flour with salt. Add half of the extra virgin olive oil and lukewarm water. Stir with a spoon and form a dough ball. If the dough is too soft, add some more flour. Let the dough rest in the refrigerator for about half an hour.

2. Meanwhile, blanch the spinach, squeeze them well, and mix them with the beaten egg. Add ricotta, Parmesan, pepper, salt, nutmeg, pine nuts, and the remaining olive oil.

3. Line a low baking pan with the dough. Fill it with the spinach and ricotta mixture. Bake in a preheated oven at 180°C (356 °F) for 30-40 minutes or until the surface is golden brown.

Nutritional values: Calories: about 240 Kcal , Carbohydrates: about 15 g, Lipid: about 15 g, Proteins: about 10 g

Stuffed turkey roast with broccoli

Ingredients for 2 people:
- Turkey breast (boneless) - 400g -> Turkey breast (boneless) - 14.1 ounces
- Broccoli florets - 250g -> Broccoli florets - 8.8 ounces
- Egg white - 1
- Garlic - 1 clove
- Red chili flakes - a pinch
- Olive oil - 1 tablespoon
- Salt - to taste

Preparation:

1. In a pan, heat 1 tablespoon of olive oil and sauté the chopped garlic for a few minutes.

2. Add the broccoli florets, previously boiled in salted water and drained, along with the red chili flakes. Cook for a few minutes until well-flavored. Turn off the heat and let it cool. Then, add the egg white and mix well.

3. On the working surface, flatten the turkey breast, cut a lateral pocket, and stuff it with the broccoli mixture. Seal it with kitchen twine, brush with the remaining oil, and bake at 180°C (356°F) for 40 minutes, turning it once. If necessary, moisten with a little broth.

4. Remove from the oven, let it rest for a few minutes, then slice and serve it hot.

Nutritional values: Calories: about 277 Kcal , Carbohydrates: about 7 g, Lipid: about 14 g, Proteins: about 53 g

Millet, vegetable, and turmeric pattie

Ingredients for 2 people:

- 100 grams of millet -> about 3.5 ounces of millet
- 1/2 bell pepper
- 1 zucchini
- 1/2 eggplant
- 1/2 carrot
- 1 egg
- A pinch of iodized salt
- Red pepper flakes to taste
- Turmeric to taste
- 1 tablespoon of extra virgin olive oil
- 1/2 tablespoon of sesame seeds

Preparation:

1. Cook the millet on low heat in boiling salted water (one part millet to two parts water) until the water is absorbed and the millet is cooked.
2. Meanwhile, cook the diced vegetables with red pepper flakes in 2 tablespoons of extra virgin olive oil.
3. Mix the millet with the vegetables, quickly sautéing in the pan. Then, add the egg and turmeric. Let it rest and cool for 20 minutes in the fridge.
4. Once well-cooled and compact, remove from the fridge, shape small patties, and coat them in sesame seeds. Bake in the oven at 180°C (356 °F)for 15/20 minutes, turning them at least once.

Nutritional values: Calories: about 286 Kcal , Carbohydrates: about 39 g, Lipids: about 19.4 g, Proteins: about 13.5g

Chicken strips with cherry tomatoes and arugula

Ingredients for 2 people:

- 400g chicken strips -> 14.1 ounces chicken strips
- 10 cherry tomatoes
- Balsamic vinegar to taste
- Extra virgin olive oil to taste
- Salt to taste
- A sprinkle of pepper

Preparation:

1. Start by taking a bunch of rosemary, chop the needles with a knife, and pour them into a slightly moistened non-stick pan.
2. Prepare the cherry tomatoes by washing them under running water, removing any leaves, and dividing them into four parts.
3. Place a medium-sized pan on the stove, heat some extra virgin olive oil, and add the cherry tomatoes. Sauté them for a few minutes, season with salt, cover with a lid, and continue cooking for a few more minutes, stirring them several times with a wooden spoon.
4. Add the chicken strips, cut into rather irregular pieces. Cook them for no more than a minute per side, then add salt, sprinkle with freshly ground pepper, and splash with half a glass of dry white wine or a decent amount of balsamic vinegar.
5. After letting the liquid evaporate, turn off the heat, remove the pan from the stove, and add the arugula, previously cleaned and torn into small pieces (if preferred, arugula can be added as whole leaves).
6. Serve the warm chicken, garnishing with shavings of Parmesan.

Nutritional values: Calories: about 250 Kcal , Carbohydrates: about 10 g, Lipid: about 20 g, Proteins: about 30 g

41

Grilled chicken salad with avocado and spinach

Ingredients for 2 people:

- 200 g chicken breast, grilled and sliced (7 oz)
- 100 g fresh spinach (3.5 oz)
- 1 avocado, sliced
- 1 medium cucumber, sliced
- 1 medium tomato, chopped
- 30 g feta cheese, crumbled (1 oz)
- 2 tbsp olive oil
- 1 tbsp balsamic vinegar
- Salt and pepper to taste

Preparation:

1. Arrange the spinach, cucumber, and tomato on two plates.
2. Top with grilled chicken slices, avocado, and feta cheese.
3. Drizzle with olive oil and balsamic vinegar.
4. Season with salt and pepper to taste.

Nutritional values: Calories: 350 Kcal , Carbohydrates: 12 g, Lipid: 24 g, Proteins: 25 g

Gratin baked fresh tuna

Ingredients for 2 people:

- 4 fresh tuna fillets (cut somewhat thick)
- 200g breadcrumbs-> 7.1 ounces breadcrumbs
- Onion
- 1 anchovy
- A bunch of parsley
- Extra virgin olive oil

Preparation:

1. In a food processor, finely chop all the ingredients: parsley, onion, and anchovy. Pour the mixture into a bowl, add a little olive oil, mix everything with your hands, and coat the tuna fillets with the breadcrumbs, ensuring the fish is completely covered.
2. Place each tuna fillet in a baking dish greased with a little oil.
3. Bake for 15 minutes at 200°C (392 °F).

Nutritional values: Calories: about 240 Kcal , Carbohydrates: about 18 g, Lipid: about 15 g, Proteins: about 40 g

Baked beef carpaccio

Ingredients for 2 people:
- 350 g per person of Piedmontese Fassona beef, sliced for carpaccio-> 12.3 ounces per person of Piedmontese Fassona beef, sliced for carpaccio
- Aromatic herbs (sage, rosemary, mint, ...)
- A pinch of iodized salt
- 1 scant tablespoon of extra virgin olive oil

Preparation:
1. Grease the baking tray with extra virgin olive oil and arrange the beef slices.
2. Sprinkle with a pinch of iodized salt and the aromatic herbs.
3. Place it in the oven for 5 minutes at 180°C (356°F).
4. When the meat turns pink, remove the tray from the oven, season with salt, and serve hot.

Nutritional values: Calories: about 350 Kcal , Carbohydrates: about 0 g, Lipid: about 22 g, Proteins: about 35 g

Anchovy and vegetable tart

Ingredients for 2 people:
- 250 g fresh anchovies -> 8.8 ounces fresh anchovies
- 150 g Swiss chard leaves -> 5.3 ounces Swiss chard leaves
- 100 g borage -> 3.5 ounces borage
- 12.5 g grated cheese -> 0.44 ounces grated cheese
- 1/2 onion
- 1 egg
- 1.5 tablespoons extra virgin olive oil
- A small bunch of parsley, basil, and marjoram
- 1 garlic clove
- 1/2 tablespoon breadcrumbs
- A pinch of iodized salt
- Pepper to taste

Preparation:
1. Clean and bone the anchovies. Wash the Swiss chard and borage leaves and cut them into pieces.
2. Cook them for a few minutes in boiling salted water, drain them, and roughly chop them.
3. Chop the onion and sauté it in a pan with 1.5 tablespoons of extra virgin olive oil, adding the chopped vegetables to enhance their flavor.
4. Season with pepper and iodized salt, then let it cool.
5. In a bowl, mix the vegetables with eggs, grated cheese, chopped herbs, and garlic.
6. Line the bottom of a 24 cm (9,44 inches) baking tray with parchment paper. Alternate layers of anchovies and vegetables in four layers, starting with the radiantly arranged anchovies.
7. Place the remaining anchovies on the top layer and sprinkle with breadcrumbs and parsley. Finally, drizzle with 0.5 tablespoons of extra virgin olive oil.
8. Bake in a preheated oven at 100°C (356°F) for 30 minutes.

Nutritional values: Calories: about 400 Kcal , Carbohydrates: about 12 g, Lipid: about 20 g, Proteins: about 40 g

Eggless chickpea and jerusalem artichoke frittata

Ingredients for 2 people:

- 50 g chickpea flour -> 1.76 ounces chickpea flour
- 150 g Jerusalem artichokes -> 5.29 ounces Jerusalem artichokes
- 150 ml water -> 5.07 fluid ounces water
- 1 sachet saffron
- 1 sprig of rosemary
- 1 tablespoon extra virgin olive oil
- A pinch of iodized salt

Preparation:

1. Dissolve saffron in 3 tablespoons of hot water, then mix it with cold water until you reach 150 ml.
2. Place chickpea flour in a bowl and slowly add saffron-infused water, stirring with a whisk to obtain a liquid batter. Cover and let it rest for about 2 hours.
3. Thoroughly clean the Jerusalem artichokes, slice them thinly using a mandoline, and place them in a bowl, covering them with cold water.
4. Line a low-rimmed baking tray of 28 or 30 cm (11,02- 11,81 inches) with previously dampened and squeezed parchment paper.
5. Drain the Jerusalem artichokes, dry them, and season with 1 tablespoon of extra virgin olive oil, rosemary, and a pinch of iodized salt. Mix them with the chickpea batter and pour into the tray.
6. Bake at 220°C (428°F) for about 20 minutes until a golden crust forms.
7. Let it rest for 10 minutes before serving.

Nutritional values: Calories: about 200 Kcal , Carbohydrates: about 30 g, Lipid: about 6 g, Proteins: about 5 g

Acquese-style stockfish

Ingredients for 2 people:

- 250 g soaked stockfish -> 8.82 ounces soaked stockfish
- 1.5 anchovy fillets -> 1.5 anchovy fillets
- 1 garlic clove
- 10 g pine nuts -> 0.35 ounces pine nuts
- 200 g potatoes -> 7.05 ounces potatoes
- A pinch of hot chili pepper
- A small bunch of parsley
- 25 ml dry white wine -> 1.69 tablespoons dry white wine
- Pitted olives as needed
- 1.5 tablespoons extra virgin olive oil

Preparation:

1. Wash the stockfish thoroughly and cut it into large pieces. Boil it for 15 minutes in unsalted water and let it cool in its broth, carefully removing the skin and bones.
2. In a pan, pour 1.5 tablespoons of extra virgin olive oil, add finely chopped anchovy fillets and the minced garlic clove. Cook over very low heat until the anchovies completely dissolve, then add the stockfish.
3. Continue cooking, pouring in the dry white wine for 10 minutes. Add the chopped parsley with some of the pine nuts, the remaining whole pine nuts, and the pitted olives. Optionally, add a small amount of hot chili pepper. Finally, add the pre-boiled and peeled potato slices. Gently mix to avoid breaking the potatoes and let it simmer for 5 minutes.

Nutritional values: Calories: about 350 Kcal , Carbohydrates: about 20 g, Lipid: about 18 g, Proteins: about 25 g

Chicken strips with aromatic herbs and balsamic vinegar

Ingredients for 2 people:
- 250 g chicken breast (whole or sliced not too thinly) ->Approximately 8.82 ounces of chicken breast
- 1 small cup of balsamic vinegar
- Salt to taste
- 1.5 tablespoons extra virgin olive oil
- Iodized salt to taste
- A small bunch each of fresh thyme, oregano, rosemary, and sage (or an equivalent amount of dried herbs)

Preparation:
1. Wash, dry, chop, and mix all the fresh herbs together.
2. Cut the chicken into strips not too thin. In a pan, add the extra virgin olive oil and the chicken strips. Once they are well colored, add the chopped herbs and a pinch of iodized salt.
3. Bring the chicken strips to cook, adding balsamic vinegar and stirring well to let the flavors meld. Cook for a few more minutes until the cooking juices reduce, and serve hot.

Nutritional values: Calories: about 300 Kcal , Carbohydrates: about 5 g, Lipid: about 14 g, Proteins: about 35 g

Salted cod with potatoes and red pepper

Ingredients for 2 people:
- 100g softened salted cod-> Approximately 3.53 ounces of softened salted cod
- Half a dried red pepper
- 1 tablespoon sweet paprika
- 1 tablespoon olive oil
- 2 or 3 potatoes
- Quarter of a white onion
- Optional: Hot paprika (to taste)
- Salt (if necessary, based on the saltiness of the cod)

Preparation:
1. Coarsely chop the onion and place it (without oil) in a deep pan along with the cod cut into pieces, potatoes sliced into rounds, and the dried red pepper, stem and seeds removed.
2. Cover everything with a couple of glasses of water and let it cook, covered, until it reaches the desired doneness (about 20 minutes) and the desired consistency.
3. Once cooked, remove the cod from heat, add 1 tablespoon of sweet paprika and a pinch of hot paprika to your liking. Mix well to ensure the paprika dissolves.
4. Season with a tablespoon of extra virgin olive oil and serve, perhaps accompanied by toasted bread crostini.

Nutritional values: Calories: about 350 Kcal , Carbohydrates: about 45 g, Lipid: about 10 g, Proteins: about 20 g

Red onion frittata

Ingredients for 2 people:
- 200 grams weak type 00 flour> Approximately 1.6 cups of weak type 00 flour
- Approximately 200 grams of water-> Approximately 200 milliliters of water
- 1 red onion
- 1 hot chili pepper
- Olive oil
- Fine salt

Preparation:
1. In a bowl, mix water with olive oil and a pinch of salt. Gradually add the flour, stirring with a whisk until you obtain a creamy batter.
2. Slice the onion into rings and cook them in a pan with a drizzle of olive oil. Once they become tender, pour the onions into the batter and mix well.
3. Heat a pan (preferably non-stick) with a couple of tablespoons of olive oil and pour in the batter. Cook on high heat for a couple of minutes to create a crispy base. Then, cover, reduce the heat to a minimum, and let it cook for another 3-4 minutes.
4. Flip the frittata using a lid of the same size. Allow it to cook for another couple of minutes on high heat, then reduce the heat and finish cooking for an additional 3-4 minutes.
5. Serve the frittata hot, cut into pieces.

Nutritional values: Calories: about 250 Kcal , Carbohydrates: about 15 g, Lipid: about 15 g, Proteins: about 15 g

Creamy smoked salmon and cannellini soup

Ingredients for 2 people:
- 150 g smoked salmon -> Approximately 5.3 ounces of smoked salmon
- 75 g dried cannellini beans -> Approximately 2.6 ounces of dried cannellini beans
- 1 clove of garlic
- 250 mL vegetable broth -> Approximately 1 cup of vegetable broth
- 25 g grated Parmesan cheese -> Approximately 0.9 ounces of grated Parmesan cheese
- 1 tablespoon extra virgin olive oil
- A small bunch of fresh chervil
- Salt, to taste
- Pepper, to taste

Preparation:
1. Place the cannellini beans in a container, covered with cold water, preferably the night before, to rehydrate them.
2. Heat the olive oil with the garlic clove (which will be removed later) in a pot, then add the well-drained cannellini beans.
3. Stir and cover with cold water, bring to a boil, and cook for about an hour and a half.
4. Blend everything into a smooth cream.
5. If needed, add some hot broth to make the mixture smoother and adjust the salt.
6. Plate the cream in individual servings, place a tuft of smoked salmon in the center, a handful of fresh pepper, two or three tufts of chervil, and a drizzle of extra virgin olive oil.

Nutritional values: Calories: about 300 Kcal , Carbohydrates: about 20 g, Lipid: about 15 g, Proteins: about 20 g

Stuffed squid with porcini mushrooms

Ingredients for 2 people:

- 100 g squid -> Approximately 3.5 ounces of squid
- 100 g porcini mushrooms -> Approximately 3.5 ounces of porcini mushrooms
- 50 g of stale bread -> Approximately 1.8 ounces of stale bread
- 4 g parsley-infused oil -> Approximately 1 teaspoon of parsley-infused oil
- Salt and pepper to taste

Preparation:

1. Clean the squid under running water, detach the tentacles and head from the body, and remove the internal cartilage, viscera, and skin, being careful not to break it.
2. Cut the squid tentacles, external fins, and porcini mushrooms into small pieces. Cook them all together in a pan with parsley-infused oil, salt, and pepper, adding the stale bread afterward.
3. Stuff the squid body with the mixture and bake for 10 minutes at 180 °C (356 °F).
4. For optimal results, avoid overfilling the squid

Nutritional values: Calories: about 150 Kcal , Carbohydrates: about 20 g, Lipid: about 5 g, Proteins: about 10 g

Cabbage with cannellini

Ingredients for 2 people:

- 600 g cabbage -> Approximately 1.3 pounds of cabbage
- 320 g dried cannellini beans, soaked overnight -> Approximately 11.3 ounces of dried cannellini beans, soaked overnight
- 3-4 cloves of garlic, chopped
- 1 sprig of rosemary
- Chili flakes
- Extra virgin olive oil
- Salt to taste

Preparation:

1. Boil cabbage and soaked cannellini beans separately in boiling water. Drain the beans when they are al dente.
2. Drain the cabbage and coarsely chop it. In a large pan, sauté garlic, chili flakes, and rosemary in olive oil.
3. Let it brown, then add the cabbage and beans to the pan.
4. Add salt, mix, and finish cooking.

Nutritional values: Calories: about 350 Kcal , Carbohydrates: about 60 g, Lipid: about 2 g, Proteins: about 20 g

Lamb stew with cardoons

Ingredients for 2 people:
- 360 g lamb -> Approximately 0.8 pounds of lamb
- 160 g cardoons -> Approximately 5.6 ounces of cardoons
- 0.25 g sage -> A pinch of sage
- 0.25 g rosemary -> A pinch of rosemary
- 8 g extra virgin olive oil -> Approximately 1.5 teaspoons of extra virgin olive oil
- 39.6 g red wine (40 ml) -> Approximately 1.4 fluid ounces of red wine (40 ml)
- 4 g garlic (1 clove) -> 1 clove of garlic
- 0.5 g salt -> A pinch of salt

Preparation:
1. Heat the olive oil in a non-stick pan and brown the lamb cubes with garlic, sage, rosemary, and previously cleaned and washed cardoons.
2. Add the wine and let it simmer for 10 minutes. Then add salt and a cup of hot water, and let it cook for another 40 minutes.

Nutritional values: Calories: about 540 Kcal , Carbohydrates: about 5 g, Lipid: about 35 g, Proteins: about 40 g

Stuffed sardines with orange and pine nuts

Ingredients for 2 people:
- 300 g sardines -> Approximately 10.5 ounces of sardines
- 50 g breadcrumbs -> Approximately 1.75 ounces of breadcrumbs
- 10 g pine nuts -> Approximately 0.35 ounces of pine nuts
- 15 g sultana raisins (soaked for about 30 minutes) -> Approximately 0.5 ounces of sultana raisins (soaked for about 30 minutes)
- Juice of 1/4 orange
- A bunch of parsley
- 15 ml extra virgin olive oil -> Approximately 1 tablespoon of extra virgin olive oil
- A few bay leaves
- 1 clove garlic
- 1 stalk chives
- 3 cherry tomatoes
- Salt and pepper to taste

Preparation:
1. Clean the sardines, removing scales, gutting, and removing the head and spine. Wash and dry them, then gently open them like a book without separating the two halves.
2. In a non-stick pan, brown the breadcrumbs, stirring continuously and being careful not to burn them.
3. In a bowl, combine breadcrumbs, chopped parsley, garlic, chives, soaked raisins, pine nuts, diced cherry tomatoes, salt, and pepper. Mix well.
4. In a baking dish, place bay leaves on the bottom, lay the sardines, sprinkle them with the mixture, then roll them up into rolls (keeping the skin on the outside).
5. Season with extra virgin olive oil and orange juice, and decorate with bay leaves.
6. Bake in a preheated oven at 190°C (374 °F) for about 20-25 minutes.

Nutritional values: Calories: about 480 Kcal , Carbohydrates: about 30 g, Lipid: about 26 g, Proteins: about 30 g

Grilled lemon chicken

Ingredients for 2 people:
- 200g chicken breast -> Approximately 7 ounces of chicken breast
- 60g breadcrumbs -> Approximately 2.1 ounces of breadcrumbs
- Lemon juice, as needed
- Mint, as needed
- Parsley, as needed
- Salt and pepper, as needed

Preparation:
1. Place the chicken breast on a chopping board and flatten it with a meat mallet to soften the meat and reduce its thickness.
2. Squeeze some lemons and pour the juice into a shallow dish, then immerse the chicken slices in it.
3. In a bowl, combine chopped parsley and mint, breadcrumbs, salt, and pepper.
4. Preheat the grill over medium heat. Meanwhile, coat the chicken breast with the breadcrumb mixture, ensuring the breadcrumbs and herbs adhere well.
5. Grill the chicken, turning it several times, until the breadcrumbs are well-grilled on both sides.

Nutritional values: Calories: about 320 Kcal , Carbohydrates: about 20 g, Lipid: about 10 g, Proteins: about 35 g

Pike with polenta

Ingredients for 2 people:
- Pike, about 500g -> Pike, about 1.1 pounds
- Anchovy fillets, 10g -> Anchovy fillets, about 0.35 ounces
- Capers, 20g -> Capers, about 0.7 ounces
- Chopped parsley
- Bay leaves
- Vegetables of choice
- 1 shot glass of vinegar
- 70g extra virgin olive oil -> Approximately 2.5 ounces of extra virgin olive oil

Ingredients for polenta:
- Cornmeal, 100g
- Water, 750ml

Preparation:
1. Cut the head and tail of the pike. Use them to prepare a fish broth by placing them in a pot of cold water with vegetables (e.g., a carrot, a piece of onion, celery), bay leaves, a splash of vinegar, and a pinch of salt. Boil for about 20-30 minutes.
2. Strain the fish broth with a colander and bring it back to a boil. Cut the remaining pike into 3 pieces and cook it in the prepared broth for about 20-40 minutes, depending on size.
3. Prepare the sauce by cooking and combining in a pan for a few minutes: olive oil, anchovies, the remaining vinegar, bay leaves, and capers.
4. Once the pike is cooked, debone and remove the skin, then season it with the sauce. Let it rest in the refrigerator, covered with plastic wrap, for about 12 hours.

Preparation for polenta:
5. In a pot with high sides, bring the water to a boil.
6. Once boiling, add salt and slowly pour in the cornmeal while stirring with a wooden spoon or whisk.
7. Once it returns to a boil, cook over low heat for at least 60 minutes, stirring frequently and being careful not to let it stick.

Nutritional values: Calories: about 550 Kcal , Carbohydrates: about 35 g, Lipid: about 28 g, Proteins: about 30 g

Trout in sweet and sour sauce

Ingredients for 2 people:
- Trout, about 300g (cleaned) -> Trout, about 10.5 ounces (cleaned)
- 1 medium white onion
- 2 tablespoons pine nuts
- 1 tablespoon chopped parsley
- 7.5 tablespoons dry white wine -> Approximately 3/8 cup dry white wine
- 1 bay leaf
- 7.5 tablespoons white vinegar -> Approximately 3/8 cup white vinegar
- 1.5 cherry tomatoes
- 5 tablespoons extra virgin olive oil -> Approximately 1/4 cup plus 1 tablespoon extra virgin olive oil
- Salt and pepper

Preparation:
1. Preheat the oven and place the salted and peppered trout with a drizzle of olive oil for 15 minutes.
2. Once cooked, remove it from the oven, debone, and place the flesh on a serving plate.
3. Slice the onions thinly, put them in a pan with a little oil, and braise them over low heat to soften. Add the bay leaf and pine nuts.
4. Pour white wine and vinegar, cook for 15 minutes. Pour the mixture over the trout, sprinkle with chopped parsley, and garnish with halved cherry tomatoes. Cover with a drizzle of olive oil.
5. Serve the appetizer at room temperature. It pairs well with fresh polenta or toasted slices of homemade bread.
6. It's recommended to prepare the dish a day in advance to enhance the flavors. Can also be served as a main course.

Nutritional values: Calories: about 450 Kcal , Carbohydrates: about 15 g, Lipid: about 30 g, Proteins: about 25 g

Milk-braised cod

Ingredients for 2 people:
- Codfish, about 300g (soaked) -> Codfish, about 10.5 ounces (soaked)
- 2 tablespoons white flour
- 1 medium white onion
- 50g salted anchovies -> Approximately 1.75 ounces salted anchovies
- 125ml milk -> Approximately 4.2 fluid ounces milk
- 3 tablespoons extra virgin olive oil
- 1.5 tablespoons chopped parsley
- 2 bay leaves
- Salt (moderation), pepper

Preparation:
1. Cut the well-drained and dried cod fillets into pieces.
2. Separately, slice the onion thinly, wash and bone the salted anchovies, and prepare the extra virgin olive oil.
3. Sauté the ingredients over low heat in a preferably non-stick pan.
4. Coat the cod fillets with flour, add salt and pepper, and place them in the pan with anchovies and onions. Increase the heat for a few minutes, turn the fillets to flavor them on both sides, and add the milk and bay leaves.
5. Slowly cook for 2 hours, adding more milk if necessary.
6. Once cooked, serve the cod on a well-heated serving plate with a sprinkle of chopped parsley and a drizzle of extra virgin olive oil. Accompany with slices of toasted polenta.

Nutritional values: Calories: about 450 Kcal , Carbohydrates: about 15 g, Lipid: about 20 g, Proteins: about 40 g

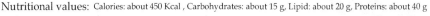

Cuttlefish stew with peas, porcini mushrooms, and anchovies

Ingredients for 2 people:

- 400g cuttlefish -> Approximately 14.11 ounces
- 1 bunch of parsley
- 1 clove of garlic
- 7.5g dried porcini mushrooms -> Approximately 0.26 ounces
- 2 salted anchovies (40g) -> Approximately 1.41 ounces
- 1/4 cup dry white wine (80g) -> Approximately 2.82 ounces
- 40g extra virgin olive oil -> Approximately 1.41 ounces
- 1 tablespoon tomato paste (20g) -> Approximately 0.71 ounces
- A handful of pine nuts (20g) -> Approximately 0.71 ounces
- 200g peas -> Approximately 7.05 ounces

Preparation:

1. Wash, clean, and cut cuttlefish into strips.
2. Soak dried porcini mushrooms in lukewarm water, then squeeze and chop them.
3. Cut 1 clove of garlic and a bunch of parsley.
4. Remove the bones from 2 salted anchovies and coat them with extra virgin olive oil.
5. Place the cuttlefish in a preferably terracotta pot, add the chopped garlic and parsley, and sauté.
6. Pour white wine into the pot. Once the alcohol has evaporated, add the chopped mushrooms and tomato paste, previously diluted in warm water.
7. Season with salt and cook for about 30 minutes. Towards the end of cooking, add peas and pine nuts.

Nutritional values: Calories: about 400 Kcal, Carbohydrates: about 10 g, Lipid: about 17 g, Proteins: about 34,6 g

CHAPTER 6: SIDE DISHES

Warm savoy cabbage salad

Ingredients for 2 people:
- 1/2 small Savoy cabbage
- Anchovies to taste
- 15 grams of extra virgin olive oil -> Approximately 1 tablespoon
- White or apple vinegar to taste
- Iodized salt to taste
- Pepper to taste

Preparation:
1. Finely chop the Savoy cabbage and place it in a bowl.
2. Season it with chopped anchovies, extra virgin olive oil, vinegar, iodized salt, and pepper.
3. Place the bowl over a pot of boiling water for about 15 minutes and serve warm.

Nutritional values: Calories: about 66,5 Kcal , Carbohydrates: about 11 g, Lipid: about 8,3 g, Proteins: about 3,25 g

Salad with walnuts and green apple

Ingredients for 2 people:
- 50g insalatina novella-> Approximately 1.76 ounces
- 1 Granny Smith apple
- 4 walnuts
- 1 tablespoon extra virgin olive oil
- Balsamic vinegar, to taste
- Iodized salt, to taste

Preparation:
1. Clean the insalatina novella.
2. Peel and cut the apple into cubes.
3. Shell and crush the walnuts.
4. Mix the ingredients and season everything with extra virgin olive oil, balsamic vinegar, and iodized salt according to your taste.

Nutritional values: Calories: about 210 Kcal , Carbohydrates: about 17 g, Lipid: about 15 g, Proteins: about 2 g

Grilled vegetables with yogurt sauce

Ingredients for 2 people:
- 1 Medium Zucchini
- 1 Medium Eggplant
- 1 Red Bell Pepper
- 1 Yellow Bell Pepper
- 50g Green Bell Pepper-> Approximately 1.76 ounces
- 1 Radicchio or Escarole or Belgian Endive
- 1 Lemon
- Small Bunch of Chopped Parsley
- Small Bunch of Chives
- Extra Virgin Olive Oil, Salt, and Pepper (to taste)
- 1 Small Container (250g- 8,81 ounces) Natural Yogurt

Preparation:
1. Slice the zucchini lengthwise, cut the eggplant into slices, divide bell peppers into wedges, and cut radicchio, escarole, or Belgian endive into wedges. Brush the various divided vegetables with oil and grill them. Season with salt and pepper to taste.
2. In a bowl, combine yogurt, lemon juice, salt, pepper, and a drizzle of olive oil. Mix everything and add the chopped chives.
3. Place the grilled vegetables on each plate and add a spoonful of the yogurt sauce.

Nutritional values: Calories: about 93,4 Kcal , Carbohydrates: about 7,9 g, Lipid: about 5,9 g, Proteins: about 2,8

Fresh spinach and mixed mushrooms

Ingredients for 2 people:
- 1 tablespoon Olive Oil
- 1 Garlic Clove
- 150g Fresh Spinach->Approximately 5,29 ounces
- Ground Pepper and Salt, to taste
- 1 tablespoon Lemon Juice

Preparation:
1. In a pan over medium-high heat, heat the olive oil. Add the crushed garlic and sauté for 10 seconds.
2. Add the mushrooms and sauté for 2 minutes.
3. Add the spinach, cover, and steam for 2-3 minutes until wilted.
4. Stir in the lemon juice, add pepper and salt to taste, and serve.

Nutritional values: Calories: about 135 Kcal , Carbohydrates: about 16 g, Lipid: about 8 g, Proteins: about 7 g

Sautéed broccoli with garlic and sun-dried tomatoes

Ingredients for 2 people:
- 500g green broccoli-> Approximately 17,63 ounces
- 1 tablespoon extra virgin olive oil
- 1 clove of garlic
- 1 sun-dried tomato
- Red chili flakes, to taste
- A pinch of iodized salt

Preparation:
1. Clean the broccoli, blanch them in boiling water for a few minutes, and drain them well.
2. Sauté the garlic, add the cut broccoli and sun-dried tomatoes.
3. Sauté for 5 minutes, adding iodized salt and chili flakes to taste.

Nutritional values: Calories: about 34 Kcal , Carbohydrates: about 4 g, Lipid: about 2 g, Proteins: about 2 g

Broccoli cream

Ingredients for 2 people:
- 250 grams of broccoli -> approximately 8.8 ounces of broccoli
- 1 tablespoon of extra virgin olive oil
- 2 anchovies
- 1/2 tablespoon of capers

Preparation:
1. Steam the broccoli until they remain bright green. Blend them with 1 tablespoon of extra virgin olive oil. Pour the obtained cream into bowls and garnish with 1 anchovy and 1 caper. Alternatively, you can also garnish with a small piece of anchovy and a sun-dried tomato cut into strips.

Nutritional values: Calories: about 87 Kcal, Carbohydrates: about 4 g, Lipids: about 8 g, Proteins: about 5 g

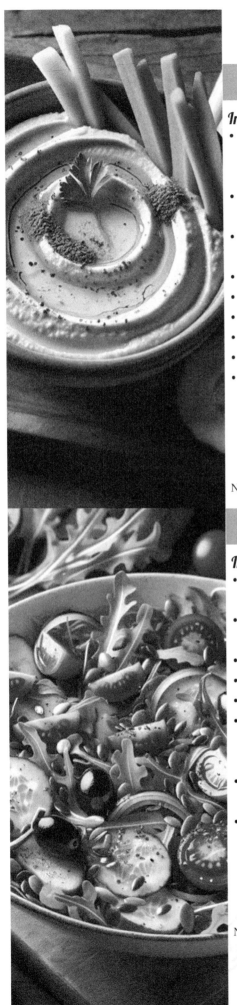

Chickpea hummus with vegetable crudité

Ingredients for 2 people:

- 200 grams of boiled chickpeas -> about 7 ounces of boiled chickpeas
- 1/2 tablespoon of tahini sesame sauce
- 1 tablespoon of extra virgin olive oil
- 1 clove of garlic
- Juice of 1 lemon
- 1 tablespoon of cumin
- Warm water as needed
- Chopped parsley as needed
- A pinch of iodized salt

Preparation:

1. In a pan, pour 1 tablespoon of extra virgin olive oil, 1 clove of garlic, and 1 tablespoon of cumin powder; then, toast everything for a couple of minutes over medium heat.
2. Add the drained chickpeas and let them flavor for another 2-3 minutes; meanwhile, squeeze the lemons and set aside their juice.
3. Transfer the chickpeas (with garlic and cumin) into a blender, add tahini and lemon juice, then blend until you obtain a smooth and homogeneous cream.
4. Add a bit of water and mix the mixture using a spoon.
5. Serve in a bowl with the vegetables, spreading chopped parsley or chili on the surface.

Nutritional values: Calories: about 181 Kcal , Carbohydrates: about 19 g, Lipids: about 23,1 g, Proteins: about 18,7 g

Arugula salad with cherry tomatoes, cucumbers, red onions, black olives, and mixed seeds

Ingredients for 2 people:

- 100g arugula->Approximately 3.5 ounces
- 60g cherry tomatoes-> Approximately 2.1 ounces.
- 1 cucumber
- 1/2 red onion
- A handful of black olives
- A handful of mixed seeds (pumpkin, flaxseed, sunflower, ...)
- 2 tablespoons extra virgin olive oil
- Iodized salt, to taste

Preparation:

1. Clean, wash, and cut the vegetables.
2. In a bowl, mix the arugula, cherry tomatoes, sliced cucumber, red onion, black olives, and mixed seeds.
3. Drizzle with extra virgin olive oil and season with iodized salt.
4. Toss everything together until well combined.
5. Serve and enjoy your refreshing salad!

Nutritional values: Calories: about 200 Kcal , Carbohydrates: about 10 g, Lipid: about 18 g, Proteins: about 6 g

Broad beans and chicory

Ingredients for 2 people:

- 120g shelled dried broad beans -> Approximately 4.23 ounces
- 500g wild chicory or Catalogna chicory -> Approximately 17.64 ounces
- 20g extra virgin olive oil (2 tablespoons)
- 1 clove of garlic
- 50g raw red onion -> Approximately 1.76 ounces
- Ground chili powder, to taste
- Salt, to taste

Preparation:

1. Soak the dried broad beans overnight.
2. Cook them for an hour in a pot with water and salt. Ensure that there's not too much water, and do not drain the beans; let the content dissolve into a sort of cream.
3. In another pot, bring lightly salted water to a boil and cook the chicory for about ten minutes. Drain and add to the pot with the broad beans.
4. Add a bit of chili powder and the clove of fresh garlic.
5. Let it all simmer for another 15 minutes. Allow it to cool for 5 minutes.
6. Plate it and add thinly sliced raw red onion and raw extra virgin olive oil.

Nutritional values: Calories: about 300 Kcal , Carbohydrates: about 47 g, Lipid: about 10 g, Proteins: about 15 g

Colored cauliflower popcorn with spices

Ingredients for 2 people:

- 350g colored cauliflower (alternatively, one whole white cauliflower) -> Approximately 12.35 ounces
- 1/2 teaspoon chopped or powdered rosemary
- 1/2 teaspoon curry and 1/4 teaspoon paprika
- 1/4 teaspoon fennel seeds
- 1/2 teaspoon thyme and 1/2 teaspoon marjoram
- Red chili flakes, to taste
- Juice of 1/2 lime
- Salt, to taste
- 10g olive oil -> Approximately 0.35 ounces

Preparation:

1. Wash the cauliflower thoroughly and divide it into popcorn-sized florets.
2. Divide the florets into four bowls and season them with a pinch of salt and 1-2 tablespoons of olive oil.
3. Flavor each bowl differently: add rosemary to one, curry and roughly chopped fennel seeds to the second, thyme and marjoram to the third, and paprika, lime juice, and a sprinkle of chili to the last one.
4. Line a baking sheet with parchment paper and spread the four types of cauliflower, keeping them separated.
5. Bake in a preheated oven at 180°C (356 °F) for 15-20 minutes.

Nutritional values: Calories: about 150 Kcal , Carbohydrates: about 20 g, Lipid: about 7,5 g, Proteins: about 5 g

CHAPTER 7: SNACK

Baked apples

Ingredients for 2 people:
- Apples: 1
- Some jam
- Puff pastry: 125g -> Approximately 4.4 ounces
- Ladyfinger (Savoiardo): 1
- Egg: 1

Preparation:
1. Peel and halve the apple, removing the core.
2. Roll out the puff pastry into a square of about 20 cm on each side. Cut 2 equal squares. Set aside the trimmings, stacked on top of each other.
3. Beat the egg and brush the edges of the squares.
4. In the center of each square, place a small piece of ladyfinger and half an apple filled with jam.
5. Fold the squares by overlapping the corners over the apple. Use the trimmings to make leaves, sticking them with the beaten egg on top.
6. After brushing the pastry, bake at 180°C (356 °F) until the puff pastry is golden brown and cooked through.

Nutritional values: Calories: about 317 Kcal , Carbohydrates: about 39,8 g, Lipid: about 16,2 g, Proteins: about 7 g

Pears in red wine

Ingredients for 2 people:
- Pears: 2
- 250 ml of red wine -> Approximately 1 cup of red wine

Preparation:
1. Peel the pears, cut them in half, and remove the cores.
2. Place them on a baking tray with the red wine.
3. Bake at 180°C (356°F) until the pears are just tender.

Nutritional values: Calories: about 153,3 Kcal , Carbohydrates: about 15 g, Lipid: about 0,2 g, Proteins: about 0,5 g

Apple and walnut cake

Ingredients for a 600g (21.16 ounces) cake:

- Delight apples: 750g ->Approximately 26.46 ounces
- All-purpose flour: 100g -> Approximately 3.53 ounces
- Whole wheat flour: 75g -> Approximately 2.65 ounces
- Butter: 75g ->Approximately 2.65 ounces
- Chopped walnut kernels: 50g -> Approximately 1.76 ounces
- Baking powder: 5g ->Approximately 0.18 ounces
- Liquid sweetener: 10g ->Approximately 0.35 ounces
- Juice of half a lemon
- Eggs: 1
- Ground cinnamon: a pinch

Preparation:

1. Place the flours on the work surface, and add the butter, egg, baking powder, and five grams of liquid sweetener.
2. Knead carefully until you obtain a crumbly but compact dough.
3. Roll out the dough to a thickness of 5-6 millimeters.
4. Place the dough in a non-stick baking pan with a diameter of about 25 cm (9,84 inches), spreading it on the bottom and sides like a box.
5. Use a special tool or fork tines to pierce the pastry to prevent it from forming bubbles.
6. Peel and core the apples, slice them thinly, and arrange them on the baking pan to cover the entire surface.
7. Sprinkle with lemon juice and the remaining liquid sweetener, and finally, spread the chopped walnut kernels.
8. Bake in an oven at a temperature of about 200°C (392 °F) for approximately three-quarters of an hour.
9. Allow it to cool before cutting into portions.

Nutritional values: Calories: about 80 Kcal , Carbohydrates: about 22 g, Lipid: about 8 g, Proteins: about 3 g

Carrot cake

Ingredients for 2 people:
- Grated medium carrots: 50g -> Approximately 1.76 ounces
- Flour: 150g -> Approximately 5.29 ounces
- Sugar: 100g -> Approximately 3.53 ounces
- Ground cinnamon: 1 teaspoon
- Corn oil: 50ml -> Approximately 1.69 fluid ounces
- Apple puree: 25ml -> Approximately 0.85 fluid ounces
- Egg whites: 3
- Walnuts: 12.5g -> Approximately 0.44 ounces
- Grated coconut: 12.5g -> Approximately 0.44 ounces
- Unsweetened canned pineapple: 25g -> Approximately 0.88 ounces
- 1/2 packet of baking powder
- 1/2 packet of vanilla sugar

For the topping:
- Fat-free Philadelphia (or similar): 75g -> Approximately 2.65 ounces
- Powdered sugar: 50g -> Approximately 1.76 ounces
- Juice of half a lemon

Preparation:
1. Preheat the oven to 180°C (356°F).
2. Boil the carrots for five minutes, drain them, and let them cool.
3. In a bowl, mix the flour, sugar, baking powder, and cinnamon.
4. In another bowl, using an electric mixer on low speed, mix the egg whites, oil, apple puree, and vanilla sugar.
5. Once the mixture is homogeneous, add the other flour-based mixture and mix well.
6. Finally, add the carrots, coconut, pineapple, and walnuts, and mix well.
7. Pour the mixture into a buttered and floured baking pan of about 30 cm (11,81 inches) in diameter. Bake for about an hour.
8. Once the cake is ready, remove it from the pan and let it cool completely.
9. In the meantime, prepare the topping by mixing the cream cheese, lemon juice, and powdered sugar with an electric mixer until the mixture is creamy.
10. Use the obtained cream to cover the cake on top and on the sides.

Nutritional values: Calories: about 390 Kcal , Carbohydrates: about 63 g, Lipid: about 12 g, Proteins: about 6 g

Orange and chocolate cake

Ingredients for a cake of approximately 800g:

- All-purpose flour: 300g -> Approximately 10.58 ounces
- Isomalt: 200g -> Approximately 7.05 ounces
- Skimmed milk: 200g -> Approximately 7.05 ounces
- Freshly squeezed orange juice: 100g -> Approximately 3.53 ounces
- Vegetable margarine: 70g -> Approximately 2.47 ounces
- Unsweetened cocoa: 50g -> Approximately 1.76 ounces
- Sweetener: 30g -> Approximately 1.06 ounces
- Baking powder: 15g -> Approximately 0.53 ounces
- Eggs: 1
- Grated orange zest

Preparation:

1. Allow the margarine to soften at room temperature.
2. Using a mixer or hand whisk, beat the margarine with the isomalt, sweetener, and egg. Add the orange zest and milk; then add the sifted flour with baking powder and cocoa.
3. Finally, add the orange juice.
4. Carefully mix all the ingredients to obtain a homogeneous and well-distributed batter, and pour it into a 24cm (9,44 inches) diameter cake tin, lightly greased and floured.
5. Bake at 180°C (356°F) for approximately 40 minutes.
6. Allow to cool and serve.

Nutritional values: Calories: about 191 Kcal , Carbohydrates: about 36 g, Lipid: about 7,5 g, Proteins: about 7 g

Chocolate ice cream

Ingredients for 2 people:
- Milk: 250g -> Approximately 8.8 fluid ounces
- Cream: 125g -> Approximately 4.4 ounces
- Isomalt: 75g -> Approximately 2.65 ounces
- Sugar: 25g -> Approximately 0.88 ounces
- Cornstarch: 20g -> Approximately 0.7 ounces
- Sweetener: 15g -> Approximately 0.53 ounces
- Eggs: 1
- Egg yolks: 1
- Low carb chocolate: 50g -> Approximately 1.76 ounces

Preparation:

1. Beat the eggs and egg yolks with isomalt and sweetener until you get a thick foam.
2. Melt the low-carb chocolate in a double boiler, mix it with cornstarch, and then add the beaten eggs and milk.
3. Cook everything over moderate heat, stirring constantly until you get a thick cream.
4. Remove from heat and add the cream, making sure to mix and blend this last mixture.
5. Put it in the ice cream maker and then in the fridge for churning.

Nutritional values: Calories: about 373 Kcal , Carbohydrates: about 86 g, Lipid: about 21 g, Proteins: about 9 g

Fried cream

Ingredients for 2 people:

- Skimmed milk: 500g -> Approximately 2 cups
- Polydextrose: 125g -> Approximately 4.4 ounces
- All-purpose flour: 120g -> Approximately 1 cup
- Breadcrumbs: 100g -> Approximately 1 cup
- Rum: 50g -> Approximately 1.76 ounces
- Powdered sweetener: 40g -> Approximately 1/4 cup
- Vanilla: 1 pinch
- Eggs: 4
- Vegetable oil for frying, as needed

Preparation:

1. Dissolve the flour, polydextrose, and two eggs in cold milk.
2. Cook the mixture until it forms a good, firm dough.
3. Remove from heat and add half of sweetener and the vanilla.
4. Moisten with rum.
5. Pour the mixture onto a lightly greased work surface and flatten it to a thickness of about one centimeter.
6. Cut the dough into diamond shapes, dip them in the remaining two eggs, and then coat them in breadcrumbs.
7. Fry in hot vegetable oil and dust with the remaining sweetener.
8. Serve hot.

Nutritional values: Calories: about 93 Kcal , Carbohydrates: about 9 g, Lipid: about 5,5 g, Proteins: about 3 g

Grapefruit carpaccio

Ingredients for 2 people:

- Grapefruit: 1.5
- Pine nuts: 1 tablespoon
- Rum: 0.5 tablespoon
- Sweetener: 2 tablespoons
- Mint

Preparation:

1. Peel the grapefruits, then remove the white membrane and seeds, and cut the fruit into circular slices.
2. Sprinkle everything with sweetener, drizzle it with rum, and let it marinate for about an hour in a cool place.
3. Mix the pine nuts, previously toasted in a non-stick pan, with the grapefruits, and add mint leaves as a garnish.

Nutritional values: Calories: about 43 Kcal , Carbohydrates: about 5 g, Lipid: about 0,6 g, Proteins: about 1 g

Strawberry bavarian cream

Ingredients for 2 people:

- Strawberries: 150g-> Approximately5.3 ounces
- Gelatin sheet
- Heavy cream: 125g-> Approximately4.4 ounces
- Sugar: 15g-> Approximately0.5 ounces

Preparation:

1. Finely chop and crush the strawberries to obtain a puree. Mix them with the gelatin sheet, previously softened with water.
2. Add sugar to the mixture and fold in the whipped cream.
3. Lightly grease a mold with oil and pour the mixture into it.
4. Refrigerate until the desired consistency is achieved. Serve the strawberry Bavarian cream chilled.

Nutritional values: Calories: about 130 Kcal , Carbohydrates: about 27,3 g, Lipid: about 98,8 g, Proteins: about 3,9 g

CHAPTER 8: RECIPES FOR VEGETARIANS

Vegetarian paella

Ingredients for 2 people:

- 150 g whole-grain rice -> Approximately 5.3 ounces
- Salt, to taste
- Approximately 1.5 tablespoons (15 ml) extra virgin olive oil
- 1 sachet of saffron
- Homemade vegetable stock: 15 g -> Approximately 0.5 ounces
- A few basil leaves
- A bunch of parsley
- 75 g bell peppers -> Approximately 2.6 ounces
- 75 g seitan -> Approximately 2.6 ounces
- 75 g carrots -> Approximately 2.6 ounces
- 75 g zucchini -> Approximately 2.6 ounces
- 75 g cherry tomatoes -> Approximately 2.6 ounces
- Shelled fresh fava beans: 75 g -> Approximately 2.6 ounces
- Approximately 375-390 ml water -> Approximately 1.6-1.7 cups
- Pepper, to taste

Preparation:

1. Bring water to a boil and season with a tablespoon of homemade vegetable stock.
2. Meanwhile, wash all the vegetables. Shell the fava beans, cut the bell pepper into wedges (after removing seeds and internal filaments), dice the zucchini and carrots, and chop the cherry tomatoes into small pieces.
3. Heat three tablespoons of oil in a large saucepan, then combine all the vegetables, except for the fava beans, adding salt and pepper to taste. Sauté the vegetables over high heat for 5 minutes.
4. Sauté the diced seitan in the pan and season with salt and pepper.
5. Rinse the whole-grain parboiled rice and add it to the vegetables. Add the fava beans and mix thoroughly.
6. Pour in the water, cover with the lid, and cook without stirring for about 15-20 minutes.
7. Five minutes before the rice is done, dissolve a sachet of saffron in a tablespoon of hot water and add it to the rice.
8. Turn off the heat and finish with your choice of aromatic herbs, such as parsley and basil.

Nutritional values: Calories: about 89 Kcal , Carbohydrates: about 14 g, Lipid: about 2,5 g, Proteins: about 3,4 g

Crepes pasticcio with pumpkin, zucchini, and fontina cheese

Ingredients for 2 people:

For the crepes:
- 50 g white type 00 flour -> Approximately 1.8 ounces
- 25 g whole wheat flour -> Approximately 0.9 ounces
- 10 g butter -> Approximately 0.35 ounces
- 90 g (1.5 medium) eggs
- 250 ml milk -> Approximately 1 cup
- Salt, to taste

For the filling:
- Salt, to taste
- 1 tablespoon (10 ml) extra virgin olive oil
- 100 g Fontina cheese -> Approximately 3.5 ounces
- 100 g (flesh) pumpkin -> Approximately 3.5 ounces
- 200 g (2 large) zucchini -> Approximately 7 ounces
- Pepper, to taste

Preparation:

For the crepes:
1. First, prepare the crepes by mixing both types of flour, eggs, milk, melted butter, and salt until you get a liquid, smooth batter without lumps.
2. In a hot stone pan, pour a ladle of batter; flip the pancake several times until the surface is lightly golden. Cook each crepe for a couple of minutes until you use up all the batter.

For the filling:
3. Meanwhile, prepare the filling for the crepes: cut pumpkin flesh and zucchini into small squares. Sauté the diced vegetables in a lightly oiled pan, season with salt and pepper to taste, and cook until the vegetables are tender and start to form a thick cream (about 15 minutes).
4. Meanwhile, blend the semi-soft cheese (e.g., Fontina) and set it aside in a small bowl.
5. Prepare a 26 cm (10,23 inches) diameter springform pan and line it with parchment paper. Arrange each crepe in the pan and cover it with a generous amount of vegetables; then proceed by placing a spoonful of grated semi-soft cheese. Cover again with another crepe, more filling, and cheese; continue in this way until all the ingredients are used.
6. Finish the surface of the pie by sprinkling it with a bit of cheese.
7. Bake everything in a preheated oven at 100°C (356°F) for 25-30 minutes.
8. Serve the pasticcio hot, sliced into portions.

Nutritional values: Calories: about 127 Kcal , Carbohydrates: about 9,7 g, Lipid: about 7 g, Proteins: about 7 g-

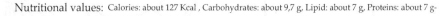

Whole wheat fresh pasta with bell peppers

Ingredients for 2 people:

- 120 g of homemade whole wheat fresh pasta -> Approximately 4.2 ounces
- 400 g of bell peppers -> Approximately 14.1 ounces or approximately 2.5 cups chopped
- 2 tablespoons of extra virgin olive oil
- A pinch of salt
- Pepper, to taste
- 1 teaspoon of sweet paprika
- 30 g of grated Grana cheese -> Approximately 1.1 ounces
- A bunch of parsley

Preparation:

1. Prepare the bell peppers by washing them in cold water, cutting them in half, and removing the stem, filaments, and seeds. Cut the cleaned peppers into matchsticks.
2. To increase the digestibility of the peppers, soak them in a solution of cold water and salt for at least 20 minutes.
3. Drain the peppers from the soaking water, rinse them under running water, and sauté them in a pan with a drizzle of olive oil, salt, pepper, and sweet paprika. Cook for about ten minutes.
4. Meanwhile, bring water to a boil, season with salt, and cook the whole wheat fresh pasta. Cook for 5 minutes or more, depending on the thickness of the pasta. If necessary, add a drop of oil to the cooking water to prevent the pasta from sticking.
5. Before the pasta is fully cooked, remove it from the water with a skimmer and finish cooking it in the pan with the bell pepper sauce.
6. Finally, add the chopped parsley and serve with a generous sprinkle of Grana cheese.
7. Serve the steaming pasta.

Nutritional values: Calories: about 122 Kcal , Carbohydrates: about 14,10 g, Lipid: about 5,5 g, Proteins: about 4,9 g

Quinoa patties with cauliflower cream and radicchio

Ingredients for 2 people:

- 100 g of quinoa -> Approximately 3.5 ounces
- About 2 tablespoons of extra virgin olive oil
- A bunch of parsley
- A pinch of chili flakes
- Salt, to taste
- Pepper, to taste
- Gluten-free product: 40-50 g of breadcrumbs -> Approximately 1.4-1.8 ounces
- 150 g of radicchio -> Approximately 5.3 ounces
- 150 g of cauliflower -> Approximately 5.3 ounces

To coat:
- Gluten-free product: About 20 g of breadcrumbs -> Approximately 0.7 ounces

Preparation:

1. First, thoroughly rinse the quinoa in cold running water.
2. Cook the quinoa in slightly salted water (the water quantity should be twice the volume of quinoa). It's recommended to add a tablespoon of oil directly to the quinoa cooking water to prevent the seeds from sticking together.
3. Meanwhile, clean the cauliflower and steam it, cutting it into small pieces to speed up the cooking time.
4. Clean the radicchio and cut it into thin strips. Sauté the radicchio in a pan, adding a drizzle of oil, salt, and pepper.
5. Pour the cauliflower into a beaker, add a drizzle of oil, salt, pepper, and a couple of tablespoons of quinoa cooking water. Blend everything with an immersion blender until you get a cream.
6. Once ready, drain the quinoa from the water and pour it into a bowl. Let it cool slightly.
7. Mix the cauliflower cream and radicchio with quinoa, stirring carefully and flavoring everything with a bit of chopped parsley.
8. If desired, add a pinch of chili flakes to the mixture.
9. At this point, gradually add the gluten-free breadcrumbs (suitable for celiacs) until you get a consistency that allows you to work the dough with your hands. You'll need of gluten-free breadcrumbs.
10. Shape the mixture into patties and roll them in gluten-free breadcrumbs.
11. Pour a drop of oil in a pan, and when it's hot, sauté the patties. They'll be ready in about 5 minutes.
12. Serve the quinoa patties on a bed of fresh radicchio.

Nutritional values: Calories: about 185 Kcal , Carbohydrates: about 25,7 g, Lipid: about 7 g, Proteins: about 6,4 g

Chickpea hummus

Ingredients for 2 people:

- 30 g chickpeas-> Approximately1 ounce
- 1 sprig of parsley
- 1 clove of garlic
- A pinch of salt
- A pinch of chili flakes
- 15-25 ml water (approximately)-> Approximately1-1.7 tablespoons
- 3 tablespoons (30 ml) extra virgin olive oil
- Unwaxed lemon juice
- 5 g (1 tablespoon) tahini

To serve:
- A few mint leaves
- A sprinkle of sweet paprika
- 1 piece of pita bread or unleavened bread

Preparation:

1. Drain the chickpeas from the soaking water and rinse them in fresh cold water to remove all antinutritional elements.
2. Plunge the chickpeas into slightly salted boiling water and cook for about an hour and a half, until tender.
3. Drain the chickpeas from the water and sauté them in a pan with a little extra virgin olive oil, a clove of garlic, and a pinch of chili flakes. If necessary, add more salt.
4. Remove the garlic clove from the chickpeas.
5. Transfer the seasoned chickpeas to a food processor, add the tahini, lemon juice, and parsley.
6. If the hummus is too thick, add some of the cooking water from the chickpeas: this will give the sauce a smoother and less compact consistency.
7. Serve the hummus (chickpea cream) with a sprinkle of sweet paprika, a few mint leaves, and pita bread.

Nutritional values: Calories: about 182 Kcal , Carbohydrates: about 12,7 g, Lipid: about 13,1 g, Proteins: about 4,1 g

Pumpkin and apple rustic cake without butter and eggs

Ingredients for 2 people:

For the dough:
- 275 g pumpkin pulp -> Approximately 9.7 ounces
- 75 g sultanas -> Approximately 2.6 ounces
- A pinch of salt
- 1 tablespoon olive oil
- 75 g (1 medium) apple -> Approximately 2.6 ounces
- 1/2 teaspoon baking powder
- 75 g whole wheat flour -> Approximately 2.6 ounces

For the topping:
- 50 ml water -> Approximately 1.7 fluid ounces
- 25 g brown sugar -> Approximately 0.9 ounces
- 150 g (about) apples -> Approximately 5.3 ounces

Preparation:

1. First, clean the pumpkin: remove the filaments and seeds from the inside and peel off the tough skin. Cut the pulp into small pieces.
2. Meanwhile, prepare the syrup, which will be used only for soaking the apples. In a saucepan, dissolve the brown sugar in boiling water. Let it cool completely, first at room temperature, then in the refrigerator.
3. Soak the sultanas in hot water for at least 10 minutes.
4. In a saucepan, heat 1 tablespoon of olive oil and sauté the pumpkin pulp. Add the softened and well-drained sultanas, along with a pinch of salt. Cook until you get a puree.
5. Meanwhile, slice the 2 apples (which will be used for decoration) into thin slices and let them soak in the cooled syrup.
6. Peel the remaining apple and cut it into small pieces. Add the apple to the pumpkin pulp, now reduced to a cream.
7. In the same pot, add the whole wheat flour and sifted baking powder.
8. Line a 24 cm diameter springform pan with parchment paper and, if necessary, use oiled hands with a tablespoon of oil to spread the dough. Neatly arrange the apple slices drained from the syrup on the surface.
9. Bake the pumpkin and apple cake in a preheated oven at 200°C (392°F) for 15 minutes. Then, reduce the temperature to 160°C (320°F) and continue for another 35 minutes.
10. Remove the cake from the oven and let it cool well before slicing.

Nutritional values: Calories: about 118 Kcal , Carbohydrates: about 25,4 g, Lipid: about 1,5 g, Proteins: about 2,2 g

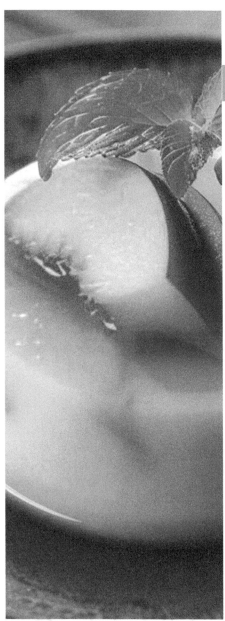

Ingredients for 2 people:

- 200 ml soy milk -> Approximately 6.8 fluid ounces
- 10 g soy flour -> Approximately 0.35 ounces
- 20 g fructose -> Approximately 0.7 ounces
- 2 g agar agar -> Approximately 0.07 ounces
- 1 vanilla pod or 1 vanilla pod extract

For the sauce (optional):

- 150 g peaches -> Approximately 5.3 ounces
- 1 tablespoon fructose
- Half a shot glass of untreated lemon juice

Preparation:

1. In a saucepan, pour the soy milk (preferably homemade) and the fructose. Heat the mixture and add the soy flour very slowly while stirring constantly with a whisk.
2. Continue stirring: a thin layer of foam will start to form. Once it reaches 80°C (176°F), add the agar agar, still stirring continuously.
3. Remove the saucepan from the heat and add the vanilla flavoring.
4. Divide the mixture into two pudding molds, optionally filtering the mixture through a strainer to remove excess foam.
5. Let the puddings cool, first at room temperature, then in the refrigerator, until they set perfectly.
6. Prepare the accompanying sauce: wash, dry, and cut the peaches into pieces. Sauté the peaches with fructose and lemon juice. Optionally, you can also flavor the peaches with a few drops of vanilla. Cook over low heat until reaching the desired consistency.
7. To remove the pudding from the mold, simply immerse the container in boiling water for a few moments and immediately flip it onto a serving plate.
8. Serve the pudding accompanied by the peach sauce.

Nutritional values: Calories: about 72 Kcal , Carbohydrates: about 13,4 g, Lipid: about 1,3 g, Proteins: about 2,5 g Calories: about 72 Kcal , Carbohydrates: about 13,4 g, Lipid: about 1,3 g, Proteins: about 2,5 g

CHAPTER 9: RECIPES FOR VEGANS

Ingredients for 2 people:

- Approximately 500 ml of vegetable broth -> Approximately 2.1 cups
- 1 or 2 tablespoons (10 or 20 ml) of extra virgin olive oil
- 150 g of pearled barley -> Approximately 5.3 ounces
- Salt, to taste
- A small bunch of parsley
- Pepper, to taste
- 1 sachet of saffron
- 200 g of zucchini -> Approximately 7 ounces

Preparation:

1. Prepare the vegetable broth by boiling salted water with a carrot, a zucchini, and a potato (alternatively, you can use vegetable broth from a cube or powder).
2. Clean and wash the zucchini thoroughly, removing any inedible parts. Cut the zucchini into small pieces and sauté them in a pan with a drizzle of extra virgin olive oil, salt, and pepper.
3. Once the zucchini are sautéed on all sides (2-3 minutes will be sufficient), pour a portion of them into a small saucepan. Add the barley and let it toast for a few minutes. The remaining portion of zucchini will be turned into a cream later.
4. At this point, proceed like a regular risotto, gradually hydrating the barley with a little hot broth at a time. The optimal cooking time for pearled barley is 30 minutes.
5. After 20 minutes, the remaining zucchini (which have completed cooking in the pan) will have softened. Pour them into a beaker and blend them into a cream with an immersion blender, adding a bit of hot broth if needed.
6. Add the zucchini cream to the pot of barley. Dissolve the saffron in a little broth, then add it to the barley.
7. Continue stirring to distribute the saffron and zucchini cream evenly. Finish cooking by flavoring with a bit of fresh parsley.
8. Optional: Arrange some grilled zucchini slices on a plate and serve immediately, garnishing with a sprig of parsley and zucchini curls.

Nutritional values: Calories: about 103 Kcal , Carbohydrates: about 18,6 g, Lipid: about 2,5 g, Proteins: about 2,7 g

Whole wheat spaghetti with lemon and walnut sauce

Ingredients for 2 people:

- 160 g of whole wheat spaghetti or whole wheat pasta -> Approximately 5.6 ounces
- 80 g of vegetable cream -> Approximately 2.8 ounces
- 50 g of walnut kernels -> Approximately 1.8 ounces
- Grated zest of an untreated lemon
- Salt, to taste
- Pepper, to taste
- A bunch of parsley

Preparation:

1. Bring a large pot of water to boil. Season with salt. Once boiling, immerse the whole wheat spaghetti and cook for 10 minutes (check the optimal cooking time on the package).
2. Meanwhile, prepare the accompanying sauce. Crush the walnuts with a suitable tool and roughly chop the kernels.
3. Heat the vegetable cream over very low heat. Grate the zest of half an organic lemon and continue stirring. Optionally, add a few drops of lemon juice for a more pronounced flavor.
4. Drain the pasta al dente and finish cooking in the cream and lemon sauce. If necessary, add a ladle of pasta cooking water; the sauce should not be too dry.
5. Chop the parsley and add it to the pasta. Serve the piping hot pasta with pepper and chopped walnut kernels.

Nutritional values: Calories: about 290 Kcal , Carbohydrates: about 25,4 g, Lipid: about 18,6 g, Proteins: about 6,7 g

Bulgur with sautéed vegetables and bell pepper cream

Ingredients for 2 people:

- 150 g of bulgur -> Approximately 5.3 ounces
- 300 ml of water -> Approximately 1.3 cups
- 200 g of zucchini -> Approximately 7 ounces
- 200 g of eggplants -> Approximately 7 ounces
- 200 g of bell peppers -> Approximately 7 ounces
- 2 tablespoons (20 ml) of extra virgin olive oil
- 1 teaspoon of sweet paprika
- A pinch of salt
- Pepper, to taste

Preparation:

1. Pour water into a small saucepan and bring it to a boil. Adjust the salt, turn off the heat, and pour the bulgur into the saucepan. Stir quickly and cover the saucepan with a lid. Let the bulgur rest for 10 minutes without stirring or lifting the lid, allowing it to absorb all the water and swell.
2. While the bulgur is cooking, prepare the vegetables. Thoroughly wash the zucchini and eggplants, remove the ends, and cut the vegetables into small cubes. Wash the bell pepper, remove the inedible parts (including seeds and filaments), and cut it into small pieces.
3. Place two pans on the heat to become very hot. In a large pan, pour zucchini and eggplants (which will serve as a condiment for bulgur), while in the other pan, place the bell peppers (which will be later blended and turned into cream). Add a dash of oil and a pinch of salt to each pan and let them cook for about ten minutes over fairly high heat.
4. Once the bell peppers are perfectly browned, reduce the heat and let them wilt for another 5 minutes. Transfer the bell peppers to a beaker and blend them with an immersion blender until a cream is formed.
5. By this time, the bulgur will have absorbed all the water. Fluff it with a spoon or fork and add it to the sautéed vegetables, with a pinch of sweet paprika.
6. Pour the bell pepper cream onto a serving plate. Place a pastry ring in the center of the sauce, then fill it with bulgur. Gently flatten the bulgur with a spoon so that it takes the shape of the mold.
7. Remove the pastry ring and serve, decorating with a little bell pepper cream, sautéed vegetables, and a sprinkle of sweet paprika.

Nutritional values: Calories: about 78 Kcal , Carbohydrates: about 14,1 g, Lipid: about 1,9 g, Proteins: about 2,1 g

Soy and rice burgers - vegan burger

Ingredients for 2 people:

- 50 g yellow soybeans -> Approximately 1.8 ounces
- 1 tablespoon olive oil
- 1/2 tablespoon soy sauce
- A pinch of salt
- 1 teaspoon sweet paprika
- A small bunch of parsley
- Some sage leaves
- About 30 g breadcrumbs -> Approximately 1.1 ounces
- About 25 ml soy milk -> Approximately 1.7 tablespoons
- 75 g carrots (1 medium) -> Approximately 2.6 ounces
- 40 g whole-grain rice -> Approximately 1.4 ounces

Optional: To serve
- Salt, to taste
- A handful of arugula
- 50 g cucumbers -> Approximately 1.8 ounces
- 50 g vine tomatoes -> Approximately 1.8 ounces
- 75 g bell peppers (1 medium) -> Approximately 2.6 ounces
- Half a shot glass of untreated lemon juice

Preparation:

1. Soak the yellow soybeans in a large bowl for 12-24 hours until they double in size.
2. Rinse the soaked soybeans in cold water, then transfer them to a saucepan filled with water (adding a pinch of salt) and cook for about 60-80 minutes until they are tender.
3. Wash and peel the carrots, then boil them in plenty of slightly salted water.
4. Also, boil the whole-grain rice in salted water for 20-30 minutes.
5. Once the soybeans, carrots, and whole-grain rice are ready, proceed to shape the burgers.
6. Pour the cooked soybeans into a blender, add the carrots and soy milk. Blend until you get a very dense mixture.
7. Pour the obtained cream into a bowl, add the boiled rice, chopped parsley, sage, soy sauce, and enough breadcrumbs to get a fairly compact mixture that can be molded with your hands.
8. Pour a layer of breadcrumbs on a flat surface and spread the mixture on it until you get a thickness of about 1.5 cm.
9. Cover again with breadcrumbs and cut out 4-5 discs by using a round pastry cutter or the edge of a cup.
10. Pour 2 tablespoons of oil into a large skillet: when hot, brown the burgers on both sides and proceed with cooking for 5 minutes.
11. Meanwhile, prepare the accompanying vegetables. Cut the bell pepper, tomato, and cucumber into cubes: season with a little salt, a little extra virgin olive oil, and a splash of lemon.
12. Serve the soy burgers with the vegetable salad and arugula leaves.

Nutritional values: Calories: about 148 Kcal , Carbohydrates: about 19,6 g, Lipid: about 5,2 g, Proteins: about 6,8 g

Veggie chickpea frittata with zucchini

Ingredients for 2 people:

- 100 g chickpea flour -> Approximately 3.5 ounces
- 150 ml water -> Approximately 5.1 fluid ounces
- 200 g zucchini -> Approximately 7 ounces
- 2 tablespoons extra virgin olive oil
- A pinch of turmeric
- 5 g flax seeds -> Approximately 0.18 ounces
- Salt, to taste
- Pepper, to taste
- A pinch of grated nutmeg

Preparation:

1. First, wash the zucchini and remove the ends. Then, cut the zucchini into small cubes or very thin slices.
2. Pour 2 tablespoons of extra virgin olive oil into a very hot skillet, then sauté the diced zucchini over high heat for a couple of minutes. Reduce the heat, adjust salt and pepper, and cook covered for about ten minutes, keeping the flame low.
3. Meanwhile, prepare the batter: in a bowl, sift the chickpea flour and add water gradually, whisking to form a dense and velvety cream, free of lumps. Adjust salt and pepper, flavor with spices of your choice (e.g., turmeric and nutmeg), and add flax seeds.
4. Add the chickpea batter directly into the zucchini pan, which by now will have a soft consistency. Maintain a lively flame for a couple of minutes, evenly distributing the mixture. Cover with the lid, reduce the flame, and cook for 7-8 minutes until the batter thickens.
5. Flip the veggie frittata onto the pan, using a flat lid: this way, a golden and inviting crust will form on both sides of the veggie frittata.
6. Serve the hot vegetable frittata.

Nutritional values: Calories: about 103 Kcal , Carbohydrates: about 13,1 g, Lipid: about 3,5 g, Proteins: about 5,5 g

Pea cheese - vegan recipe

Ingredients for 2 people:

- 25 g pea flour -> Approximately 0.9 ounces
- 62.5 g soy yogurt -> Approximately 2.2 ounces
- 1 tablespoon olive oil
- 35 ml soy milk -> Approximately 1.2 fluid ounces
- A pinch of salt
- 1/2 tablespoon pink peppercorns

Preparation:

1. In a saucepan, mix the pea flour with a pinch of salt and the pink peppercorns.
2. Pour the plain soy yogurt in the center, then add the olive oil, and gradually pour in the soy milk (unsweetened). Mix until you get a thick batter.
3. Place the saucepan on the heat and continuously stir over gentle to moderate heat until the mixture begins to thicken.
4. Allow approximately 2 minutes from the boiling point, then pour the mixture (which will appear very thick and sticky) into a cheese mold.
5. Flatten the veg-cheese with your hands or with the back of an oiled spoon and let it cool completely.
6. The veg-cheese is ready: it can be sliced and served alongside fresh vegetables.

Nutritional values: Calories: about 161 Kcal , Carbohydrates: about 16,2 g, Lipid: about 8,2 g, Proteins: about 6,7

Vegan sugar-free cookies

Ingredients for 2 people:

- 20 g whole wheat flour -> Approximately 0.7 ounces
- 10 g rolled oats -> Approximately 0.35 ounces
- 8 g stevia and erythritol blend or another type of sweetener -> Approximately 0.28 ounces
- 8 ml corn oil -> Approximately 0.27 fluid ounces
- 10 g + 2 g hazelnuts -> Approximately 0.35 + 0.07 ounces
- 10 g dates -> Approximately 0.35 ounces
- 0.8 g baking powder -> Approximately 0.03 ounces
- 10 ml water -> Approximately 0.34 fluid ounces
- A pinch of salt

Preparation:

1. In a blender, combine 10 g (0,35 ounces) of hazelnuts and the rolled oats: grind until you get a fine powder.
2. Pit the dates, cut them into pieces, and place them in the blender. Grind the dates until they form a cream.
3. In a bowl, mix the hazelnut and oat powder, whole wheat flour, sifted baking powder, salt, and the stevia and erythritol sweetener.
4. With your hands, mix the powders with the date cream until you get a crumbly mixture.
5. Now, mix everything with corn oil and water: knead with your hands to obtain a soft and non-sticky dough.
6. Wrap the dough in a sheet of plastic wrap and let it rest for half an hour.
7. Roll out the cookie dough on a flat surface using a rolling pin, optionally dusting with some whole wheat flour. Roll out the dough to about half a centimeter thick.
8. Use cookie cutters of your desired shape to cut out the cookies and place them on a baking sheet lined with parchment paper. You can rework the scraps to make more cookies.
9. Cut the remaining hazelnuts in half and place half a hazelnut in the center of each cookie.
10. Bake the cookies in a preheated oven at 180°C (356°F) for 12 minutes (for soft cookies) or for 15 minutes (for crispier cookies).
11. Remove the cookies from the oven, let them cool slightly, and serve.
12. These vegan sugar-free cookies can be stored in a tin box for 7-10 days.

Nutritional values: Calories: about 319 Kcal , Carbohydrates: about 38,8 g, Lipid: about 15,4 g, Proteins: about 8,7 g

CHAPTER 10: 60-DAY MEAL PLAN

Here's a 60-day meal plan with a variety of appetizers, first courses, second courses, side dishes, and desserts. The legume soups are alternated in the plan. Insert starters as you wish, during the 60 days of the plan:

Day 1
Breakfast: Quinoa breakfast bowl with almonds and raspberries
Lunch: Quinoa-stuffed bell peppers
Snack: Baked apples
Dinner: Ricotta and spinach whole wheat quiche with warm savoy cabbage salad

Day 2
Breakfast: Greek yogurt with berries and nuts
Lunch: Lentil soup
Snack: Pears in red wine
Dinner: Chicken strips with cherry tomatoes and arugula

Day 3
Breakfast: Oatmeal with apple and cinnamon
Lunch: Zucchini noodles with pesto and cherry tomatoes
Snack: Carrot cake
Dinner: Grilled lemon chicken with fresh spinach and mixed mushrooms

Day 4
Breakfast: Chia seed pudding with vanilla and berries
Lunch: Chickpea and leek soup

Snack: Grapefruit carpaccio
Dinner: Baked beef carpaccio with broccoli cream

Day 5
Breakfast: Cottage cheese with pineapple and flaxseeds
Lunch: Spaghetti with fresh clams
Snack: Apple and walnut cake
Dinner: Stuffed squid with porcini mushrooms

Day 6
Breakfast: Almond flour pancakes with blueberries
Lunch: Black cabbage and cannellini bean soup
Snack: Orange and chocolate cake
Dinner: Grilled lemon chicken with warm savoy cabbage salad

Day 7
Breakfast: Smoothie with spinach, banana, and peanut butter
Lunch: Lentil and vegetable soup
Snack: Chocolate ice cream
Dinner: Stuffed sardines with orange and pine nuts

Day 8
Breakfast: Whole wheat toast with avocado and strawberry
Lunch: Artichokes in rice salad
Snack: Strawberry bavarian cream
Dinner: Chicken strips with aromatic herbs and balsamic vinegar

Day 9
Breakfast: Ciambellone (Italian ring cake)
Lunch: Pasta and cauliflower minestrone
Snack: Baked apples
Dinner: Trout in sweet and sour sauce with sautéed broccoli

Day 10
Breakfast: Cocoa and raspberry pancakes
Lunch: Spaghetti with anchovies sauce
Snack: Pears in red wine
Dinner: Milk-braised cod with arugula salad

Day 11
Breakfast: Baked sweet milk
Lunch: Lentil soup
Snack: Carrot cake
Dinner: Eggless chickpea and Jerusalem artichoke frittata with chickpea hummus

Day 12
Breakfast: Vanilla yogurt and strawberry pudding
Lunch: Risotto with cuttlefish and mushrooms
Snack: Grapefruit carpaccio
Dinner: Grilled lemon chicken with grilled vegetables

Day 13
Breakfast: Quinoa breakfast bowl with almonds and raspberries
Lunch: Chickpea and leek soup
Snack: Apple and walnut cake
Dinner: Anchovy and vegetable tart with warm savoy cabbage salad

Day 14
Breakfast: Greek yogurt with berries and nuts
Lunch: Spaghetti with cob sauce
Snack: Orange and chocolate cake
Dinner: Pike with polenta

Day 15
Breakfast: Oatmeal with apple and cinnamon
Lunch: Lentil soup
Snack: Strawberry bavarian cream
Dinner: Stuffed sardines with orange and pine nuts

Day 16
Breakfast: Cottage cheese with pineapple and flaxseeds
Lunch: Whole wheat spaghetti with tomato and spinach
Snack: Chocolate ice cream
Dinner: Chicken strips with cherry tomatoes and arugula

Day 17
Breakfast: Almond flour pancakes with blueberries
Lunch: Borlotti bean soup
Snack: Grapefruit carpaccio
Dinner: Grilled lemon chicken with fresh spinach and mixed mushrooms

Day 18
Breakfast: Smoothie with spinach, banana, and peanut butter
Lunch: Spaghetti squash with marinara
Snack: Carrot cake
Dinner: Salted cod with potatoes and red pepper

Day 19
Breakfast: Quinoa breakfast bowl with almonds and raspberries
Lunch: Mixed cereal and legume soup
Snack: Baked apples
Dinner: Gratin baked fresh tuna with broccoli cream

Day 20

Breakfast: Greek yogurt with berries and nuts
Lunch: Minestrone with legumes
Snack: Pears in red wine
Dinner: Eggless chickpea and Jerusalem artichoke frittata with salad

Day 21

Breakfast: Ciambellone (Italian ring cake)
Lunch: Pasta and cauliflower minestrone
Snack: Orange and chocolate cake
Dinner: Chicken strips with aromatic herbs and balsamic vinegar

Day 22

Breakfast: Cocoa and raspberry pancakes
Lunch: Spelt salad with peppers and zucchini
Snack: Strawberry bavarian cream
Dinner: Pike with polenta

Day 23

Breakfast: Baked sweet milk
Lunch: Black cabbage and cannellini bean soup
Snack: Carrot cake
Dinner: Stuffed turkey roast with broccoli

Day 24

Breakfast: Vanilla yogurt and strawberry pudding
Lunch: Linguine with zucchini, thyme, and lemon
Snack: Grapefruit carpaccio
Dinner: Milk-braised cod with arugula salad

Day 25

Breakfast: Quinoa breakfast bowl with almonds and raspberries
Lunch: Lentil soup
Snack: Apple and walnut cake
Dinner: Grilled lemon chicken with warm savoy cabbage salad

Day 26

Breakfast: Greek yogurt with berries and nuts
Lunch: Artichokes in rice salad
Snack: Baked apples
Dinner: Trout in sweet and sour sauce with sautéed broccoli

Day 27

Breakfast: Oatmeal with apple and cinnamon
Lunch: Quinoa-stuffed bell peppers
Snack: Strawberry bavarian cream
Dinner: Ricotta and spinach whole wheat quiche with salad

Day 28

Breakfast: Chia seed pudding with vanilla and berries
Lunch: Chickpea and leek soup
Snack: Orange and chocolate cake
Dinner: Grilled lemon chicken with fresh spinach and mixed mushrooms

Day 29

Breakfast: Cottage cheese with pineapple and flaxseeds
Lunch: Spaghetti with fresh clams
Snack: Grapefruit carpaccio
Dinner: Chicken strips with cherry tomatoes and arugula

Day 30

Breakfast: Almond flour pancakes with blueberries
Lunch: Lentil and vegetable soup
Snack: Carrot cake
Dinner: Stuffed squid with porcini mushrooms

Day 31

Breakfast: Smoothie with spinach, banana, and peanut butter
Lunch: Risotto with cuttlefish and mushrooms
Snack: Apple and walnut cake

Dinner: Grilled lemon chicken with warm savoy cabbage salad

Day 32
Breakfast: Quinoa breakfast bowl with almonds and raspberries
Lunch: Borlotti bean soup
Snack: Baked apples
Dinner: Baked beef carpaccio with broccoli cream

Day 33
Breakfast: Greek yogurt with berries and nuts
Lunch: Pasta and cauliflower minestrone
Snack: Strawberry bavarian cream
Dinner: Salted cod with potatoes and red pepper

Day 34
Breakfast: Cocoa and raspberry pancakes
Lunch: Chickpea pasta with lemon and broccoli
Snack: Carrot cake
Dinner: Eggless chickpea and Jerusalem artichoke frittata with chickpea hummus

Day 35
Breakfast: Baked sweet milk
Lunch: Spelt salad with peppers and zucchini
Snack: Grapefruit carpaccio
Dinner: Pike with polenta

Day 36
Breakfast: Vanilla yogurt and strawberry pudding
Lunch: Minestrone with legumes
Snack: Apple and walnut cake
Dinner: Chicken strips with aromatic herbs and balsamic vinegar

Day 37
Breakfast: Ciambellone (Italian ring cake)
Lunch: Spaghetti with cob sauce
Snack: Orange and chocolate cake

Dinner: Ricotta and spinach whole wheat quiche with salad

Day 38
Breakfast: Cocoa and raspberry pancakes
Lunch: Spelt salad with peppers and zucchini
Snack: Strawberry bavarian cream
Dinner: Pike with polenta

Day 39
Breakfast: Baked sweet milk
Lunch: Minestrone with legumes
Snack: Apple and walnut cake
Dinner: Chicken strips with aromatic herbs and balsamic vinegar

Day 40
Breakfast: Vanilla yogurt and strawberry pudding
Lunch: Quinoa-stuffed bell peppers
Snack: Grapefruit carpaccio
Dinner: Stuffed turkey roast with broccoli

Day 41
Breakfast: Quinoa breakfast bowl with almonds and raspberries
Lunch: Lentil soup
Snack: Strawberry bavarian cream
Dinner: Stuffed sardines with orange and pine nuts

Day 42
Breakfast: Cottage cheese with pineapple and flaxseeds
Lunch: Whole wheat spaghetti with tomato and spinach
Snack: Chocolate ice cream
Dinner: Chicken strips with cherry tomatoes and arugula

Day 43
Breakfast: Almond flour pancakes with blueberries

Lunch: Borlotti bean soup
Snack: Grapefruit carpaccio
Dinner: Grilled lemon chicken with fresh spinach and mixed mushrooms

Day 44
Breakfast: Smoothie with spinach, banana, and peanut butter
Lunch: Spaghetti squash with marinara
Snack: Carrot cake
Dinner: Salted cod with potatoes and red pepper

Day 45
Breakfast: Quinoa breakfast bowl with almonds and raspberries
Lunch: Mixed cereal and legume soup
Snack: Baked apples
Dinner: Gratin baked fresh tuna with broccoli cream

Day 46
Breakfast: Greek yogurt with berries and nuts
Lunch: Lentil and vegetable soup
Snack: Pears in red wine
Dinner: Eggless chickpea and Jerusalem artichoke frittata with salad

Day 47
Breakfast: Oatmeal with apple and cinnamon
Lunch: Artichokes in rice salad
Snack: Orange and chocolate cake
Dinner: Grilled lemon chicken with warm savoy cabbage salad

Day 48
Breakfast: Chia seed pudding with vanilla and berries
Lunch: Pasta and cauliflower minestrone
Snack: Baked apples
Dinner: Trout in sweet and sour sauce with sautéed broccoli

Day 49
Breakfast: Cottage cheese with pineapple and flaxseeds
Lunch: Spaghetti with fresh clams
Snack: Strawberry bavarian cream
Dinner: Chicken strips with cherry tomatoes and arugula

Day 50
Breakfast: Almond flour pancakes with blueberries
Lunch: Lentil and vegetable soup
Snack: Carrot cake
Dinner: Stuffed squid with porcini mushrooms

Day 51
Breakfast: Smoothie with spinach, banana, and peanut butter
Lunch: Risotto with cuttlefish and mushrooms
Snack: Apple and walnut cake
Dinner: Grilled lemon chicken with warm savoy cabbage salad

Day 52
Breakfast: Quinoa breakfast bowl with almonds and raspberries
Lunch: Borlotti bean soup
Snack: Grapefruit carpaccio
Dinner: Baked beef carpaccio with broccoli cream

Day 53
Breakfast: Greek yogurt with berries and nuts
Lunch: Pasta and cauliflower minestrone
Snack: Strawberry bavarian cream
Dinner: Salted cod with potatoes and red pepper

Day 54
Breakfast: Cocoa and raspberry pancakes
Lunch: Chickpea pasta with lemon and broccoli
Snack: Carrot cake
Dinner: Eggless chickpea and Jerusalem

artichoke frittata with chickpea hummus

Day 55
Breakfast: Baked sweet milk
Lunch: Lentil soup
Snack: Orange and chocolate cake
Dinner: Stuffed sardines with orange and pine nuts

Day 56
Breakfast: Vanilla yogurt and strawberry pudding
Lunch: Quinoa-stuffed bell peppers
Snack: Grapefruit carpaccio
Dinner: Ricotta and spinach whole wheat quiche with salad

Day 57
Breakfast: Quinoa breakfast bowl with almonds and raspberries
Lunch: Lentil and vegetable soup
Snack: Strawberry bavarian cream
Dinner: Stuffed sardines with orange and pine nuts

Day 58
Breakfast: Greek yogurt with berries and nuts
Lunch: Artichokes in rice salad
Snack: Baked apples
Dinner: Chicken strips with cherry tomatoes and arugula

Day 59
Breakfast: Oatmeal with apple and cinnamon
Lunch: Spaghetti with fresh clams
Snack: Carrot cake
Dinner: Grilled lemon chicken with warm savoy cabbage salad

Day 60
Breakfast: Chia seed pudding with vanilla and berries
Lunch: Lentil and vegetable soup
Snack: Apple and walnut cake
Dinner: Stuffed squid with porcini mushrooms

CHAPTER 11: SHOPPING LIST

Based on the recipes listed in this book, here is a comprehensive shopping list categorized by recipe chapters.

Produce:

Almonds
Raspberries
Mixed berries (blueberries, strawberries, raspberries)
Apples
Bananas
Pineapple
Strawberries
Spinach
Avocado
Zucchini
Cherry tomatoes
Artichokes
Peas
Lettuce
Thyme
Lemons
Asparagus
Radicchio
Clams
Cauliflower
Pumpkins
Mixed mushrooms
Broccoli
Garlic
Sun-dried tomatoes
Broad beans
Chicory
Cabbage (Savoy, red cabbage)
Arugula
Cucumbers
Red onions
Mixed seeds
Cardoons
Porcini mushrooms
Chickpeas
Leeks
Cannellini beans
Borlotti beans
Various legumes
Fresh herbs (basil, parsley, dill)
Sweet potatoes
Pears
Grapefruit
Fresh tomatoes
Bell peppers
Zucchini flowers (if available)
Jerusalem artichokes

Grains and pasta:
Quinoa
Oatmeal
Chia seeds
Almond flour
Whole wheat bread
Ciambellone ingredients (flour, sugar, eggs, etc.)
Various pasta types (spaghetti, penne, linguine, tagliatelle, fusilli)
Couscous
Spelt
Black rice (Riso venere)
Rice (Arborio for risotto, other types for soups)
Bulgur
Barley

Dairy and eggs:
Greek yogurt
Cottage cheese
Ricotta
Milk (whole, almond, soy)
Eggs
Fontina cheese
Pecorino cheese

Seafood and meat:
Fresh tuna
Beef (for carpaccio)
Salted cod
Stockfish
Sardines
Cuttlefish
Shrimp
Chicken breasts
Turkey breast
Lamb

Pantry items:
Flaxseeds
Vanilla extract
Peanut butter

Olive oil
Balsamic vinegar
Mixed spices (curry, cinnamon, etc.)
Sea salt
Black pepper
Vegetable broth
Soy sauce
Various flours (whole wheat, almond)
Sugar
Baking powder
Baking soda

Nuts and seeds:
Walnuts
Mixed seeds (sunflower, pumpkin)
Pine nuts

Frozen items:
Peas (if fresh not available)

Canned and jarred goods:
Anchovies
Canned tomatoes
Tomato sauce
Artichoke hearts
Cannellini beans
Chickpeas
Borlotti beans
Stockfish

Snacks and desserts:
Chocolate (for cakes and desserts)
Ice cream (optional for dessert recipes)
Grapefruit
Apples (for baked apples)
Various cake ingredients (flour, sugar, butter, etc.)

BONUS

FREE DOWNLOAD

BONUS- Blood-Sugar-L

1. BONUS- Blood-Sugar-Log-Book_printable

BONUS- The glycemic

2. BONUS- The glycemic index table

Bonus- Food-Journal-

3. Bonus- Food-Journal-Log-Book-for-Diabetics_printable

BONUS- Dine-Out-Smar

4. BONUS- Dine-Out-Smart-A-Diabetic_s-Guide-to-Eating-Out

Bonus- WEIGHT MANAGE

5. Bonus- WEIGHT MANAGEMENT MEAL PLAN 4 WEEK PROGRAM

CONCLUSION

Understanding and managing diabetes is crucial for maintaining a healthy lifestyle. The provided index covers various aspects of diabetes, ranging from its types, diagnosis, complications, risk factors, therapeutic interventions, to the importance of adopting a diabetic diet.

KEY TAKEAWAYS:

1. **Types of Diabetes:** The index elaborates on different types of diabetes, emphasizing the need for personalized approaches in management.
2. **Diagnosis and Complications:** Clear information is presented about the diagnosis process and potential complications associated with diabetes, highlighting the importance of proactive health management.
3. **Risk Factors:** Identifying risk factors allows individuals to make informed lifestyle choices and reduce the likelihood of developing diabetes.
4. **Therapeutic Interventions:** The index introduces therapeutic interventions, acknowledging the role of both medical and dietary approaches in diabetes management.
5. **Diabetic Diet:** A significant focus is placed on the diabetic diet, explaining dietary goals, nutritional advice, and the importance of a balanced diet in managing blood sugar levels.
6. **Nutrient Distribution Throughout the Day:** Specific dietary guidelines are provided, detailing how to divide nutrients throughout the day to achieve a balanced diet.
7. **Recipes:** The inclusion of a diverse range of recipes, including appetizers, first dishes, legume soups, second dishes, side dishes, and desserts, demonstrates that a diabetic-friendly diet can be delicious, varied, and satisfying.

In summary, the comprehensive information and diverse recipe options in the index empower individuals with diabetes to make informed choices, fostering a positive approach to managing their health through nutrition. The provided recipes offer a rich and flavorful selection, promoting a diabetic diet that is not only health-conscious but also enjoyable.

ALPHABETICAL INDEX

Pasta and beans 84
Pasta and cauliflower minestrone 22
Pea cheese - vegan recipe 72
Pears in red wine 59
Penne all'arrabbiata 84
Pike with polenta 49
Pumpkin and apple rustic cake without butter and eggs 67
Pumpkin soup 33
Quinoa breakfast bowl with almonds and raspberries 15
Quinoa patties with cauliflower cream and radicchio 66
Quinoa-stuffed bell peppers 22
Red onion frittata 46
Rice, peas, and lettuce soup 84
Ricotta and spinach whole wheat quiche 40
Riso venere with cherry tomatoes and shrimp
Risotto with asparagus and peas 33
Risotto with cuttlefish and mushrooms 33
Salad with walnuts and green apple 53
Salted cod with potatoes and red pepper 45
Sautéed broccoli with garlic and sun-dried tomatoes 55
Seafood spaghetti 55
Smoothie with spinach, banana, and peanut butter 18

Soy and rice burgers – vegan burger 71
Spaghetti with anchovies sauce 31
Spaghetti with artichokes and walnuts 84
Spaghetti with cob sauce 31
Spaghetti with fresh clams 30
Spaghetti with fresh tomato 84
Spelt salad with peppers and zucchini 30
Strawberry bavarian cream 63
Stuffed sardines with orange and pine nuts 48
Stuffed squid with porcini mushrooms 47
Stuffed turkey roast with broccoli 40
Trout in sweet and sour sauce 50
Vanilla soy pudding with peach sauce 68
Vanilla yogurt and strawberry pudding 20
Vegan sugar-free cookies 73
Vegetarian paella 65
Veggie chickpea frittata with zucchini 72
Warm savoy cabbage salad 53
Whole wheat fresh pasta with bell peppers 66
Whole wheat fusilli with treviso radicchio 84
Whole wheat spaghetti with lemon and walnut sauce 70
Whole wheat toast with avocado and strawberry 18
Zucchini noodles with pesto and cherry tomatoes 23

Printed in Great Britain
by Amazon

45993086R00051